Princess Nest
of Wales *Seductress*
of the
English

About the Author

Kari Maund is a professional historian and writer, her other books include *The Welsh Kings: Warriors, Warlords & Princes* and *The Four Musketeers* both published by Tempus. She was born in Coventry and now lives in Cambridge.

Princess Nest of Wales
Seductress of the English

Kari Maund

TEMPUS

First published 2007

Tempus Publishing Limited
The Mill, Brimscombe Port,
Stroud, Gloucestershire, GL5 2QG
www.tempus-publishing.com

© Kari Maund, 2007

British Library Cataloguing in Publication Data.
A catalogue record for this book is available from the British Library.

ISBN 978 0 7524 3771 2

Typesetting and origination by Tempus Publishing Limited
Printed in Great Britain

CONTENTS

INTRODUCTION

She was the daughter of one king and the lover of another; the matriarch of a powerful dynasty and the cause of conflict and war. While most of her countrywomen lived out their lives in quiet obscurity, Nest, Princess of Dyfed, became a legend. She lived through one of the most exciting and dynamic periods of Welsh and English history, and was herself an influence upon its events. Her life provides a rare opportunity to explore the role of women in early Wales and the impact upon it of the Norman invaders.

She was born into an extraordinary time. Her father, Rhys ap Tewdwr, was king of Deheubarth, the kingdom which extended over south-west Wales, and enjoyed considerable influence throughout all Wales. Yet he had very nearly not become king at all, and throughout his reign he had the strange distinction of being the only king in Wales to hold his kingdom undisturbed by the new neighbours who were occupying England. He had become king in the early years of the Norman Conquest of England, and survived through diplomacy and the policy of William the Conqueror, but on the death of William in 1087, Norman policy changed. The new king of England, William Rufus, needed to secure the loyalty of his aristocracy with land grants and promises of booty. Casting aside the treaty forged by Rhys and his father, he allowed his barons to invade the whole of Wales. Nest, perhaps still a young child, lost her father in battle. Her brother, Gruffudd, fled into exile in Ireland, while Nest fell into the hands of the new lords of south Wales. Up to this point, she must have expected her life to follow the usual pattern for Welsh women of royal blood – marriage to an ally of her father, and a life travelling with her husband's entourage and bearing his children. The fall of Rhys changed all of this. Her captors, the earl of Shrewsbury and his son, Arnulf, the new earl of Pembroke, probably sent her into their English lands to be raised under their power.

It was a journey that would determine the rest of her life.

Despite popular modern myth, medieval Welsh women enjoyed little respect and scant freedom. Legally lifelong minors, they remained pawns in the hands of male kin, incapable of owning land and married off to suit changing political needs. Women in Anglo-Norman England enjoyed wider privileges, and Nest, the daughter of a king, probably found herself accorded an importance she had never experienced before. Under Welsh law, women were excluded from succession to royal office, and could pass only the weakest of claims on to their children. To the Normans, however, Nest was a valuable prize in the struggle to subdue south Wales. She grew into a noted beauty, and towards the end of the eleventh century she caught the eye of Prince Henry, brother and probable heir of King William Rufus. Henry could not marry her: his marriage needed to be a great alliance, and Nest had nothing like the necessary rank and status. Yet being his mistress conferred advantages of its own, and, in particular, brought her to the attention of those in power. She bore Henry a son, also named Henry, and, after he became king in 1100, he seems to have undertaken to ensure she would be maintained and looked after. He arranged her marriage to Gerald of Windsor, his steward over south Wales. As Gerald's wife, she enjoyed considerable status amongst his countrymen, while her ancestry lent him some legitimacy amongst her fellow Welsh. She returned to her homeland, where she would remain for the rest of her life, an intimate part of the complex politics which dominated it in the first decades of the twelfth century, and a cause of conflict and strife.

In 1109, she attracted the attention of Owain ap Cadwgan, figure-head of Welsh resistance to the Normans. Himself the son of a great king, Owain abducted her by night in a daring raid on her husband's castle of Cilgerran, seizing Nest and carrying her off into his lands. It was to take the intervention of Henry I himself to restore peace, but it did not last. After her abduction, Nest was to see her brother Gruffudd rise in rebellion in turn and endure the anguish of seeing her husband and sons fighting against Gruffudd and her nephews. Outliving Gerald, she was to remarry twice to Norman lords in south-west Wales, and to bear further children, all of whom rose to hold positions in the Cambro-Norman hierarchy. One of her sons became a bishop, two led the Norman invasion of Ireland, while her grandson, another Gerald, was to become one of the great historians of medieval Wales. She would be remembered by later generations both as the matriarch of a powerful clan and as a legendary beauty.

Yet, like the majority of women in this period, her life went largely unrecorded. Chroniclers, including her grandson Gerald, tell us of her sons and their deeds, but they record nothing of Nest's feelings or beliefs. Her story has to be pieced together from a patchwork of sources, written and archaeological, historical and fictional, Welsh, Anglo-Norman and English. Nest is the first woman in the history of early Wales who is more than a name in a genealogical note, frag-mentary though the extra information about her is. She lived in two worlds – the world of traditional medieval Wales and of the Norman colonists – and was a key element in the formation of a third, the Cambro-Norman society which came to exist in the marches of Wales. This book sets out to uncover as much as is possible about this extraordinary woman and the world she inhabited. It attempts to set her in all her contexts, and, through her, explore the complex political life of late eleventh- and twelfth-century Wales.

1

NEST'S WALES

Nest of Deheubarth was born at a crossroads in the history of Wales. Had her birth occurred as little as twenty years earlier, it is likely that her name would be no more to us now than a brief note in an old genealogical manuscript – someone's mother, someone's wife. But she was born in a time and place where everything was changing in Wales for men and women alike, and those changes were to bring her to the attention of an English king, an influential nobleman, a swashbuckling Welsh rebel, and to lead to at least some aspects of her life being recorded for posterity.

Early medieval Wales was in many aspects conservative, and, although its internal politics were dynamic and often dramatic, Welsh events had, up until the middle of the eleventh century, only intermittently drawn the attention or interest of their English neighbours. Although the country was much the same shape, geographically, at that time as it is now, its political map was considerably different. It was divided into several fiercely independent kingdoms, each with their own native ruling house. The number of these varied from period-to-period, as kings warred with one another, annexed or lost territories, allied, intermarried and schemed, but by Nest's time the major units were Gwynedd, in the north-west; Powys, in the north-east; Deheubarth, in the south-west; and Morgannwg, in the south-east. Nest's father, Rhys ap Tewdwr, was king of Deheubarth, then a land of good arable and grazing, forests and notable fishing resources. Its core land was the ancient kingdom of Dyfed, to which earlier kings had annexed the neighbouring territories of Ystrad Twyi, and, intermittently, Gower and Ceredigion. Nest's grandson, the writer and clergyman Gerald of Wales, was born and brought up in southern Deheubarth, in what is now Pembrokeshire, and retained a life-long love of the land. Writing in the last decades of the twelfth century, he described it as, '...a region rich in wheat, with fish from the sea and plenty of wine for sale... Of all the different parts of Wales, Dyfed with its seven cantrefs is at once the most beautiful and the most productive.'[1] In terms of the internal politics of Wales, the king of Deheubarth was one of the most powerful figures. Indeed, for much of the tenth century Wales had been dominated by a succession of effective kings from that kingdom.[2] They were Nest's ancestors, and from what we can tell, she was proud of them and their history.

What was the nature of the culture in which she spent her childhood? Society was hierarchical and heavily male dominated.[3] Our extant historical sources concentrate on the deeds of kings and their *teulu* (warbands), and upon the upper clergy; the bulk of the population – and nearly all the women – go unrecorded, outside the descriptions given in law codes, the occasional reference in a land grant or *Life* of a saint. Status was largely a matter of birth – born into a royal line, Nest herself was a member of a privileged group. Welsh kings were expected to be effective military leaders, generous patrons and upholders of the law. They seem to have been semi-nomadic, travelling about their kingdoms, visiting both their own estates and those of their aristocracy and clergy. They were accompanied in this by their warband, which was made up of young noblemen and royal kinsmen, as well as by their immediate family and the royal household of servants and officials. This peripatetic lifestyle allowed them to monitor continuously the mood of their country, and to keep a close eye on their people. Also, it served another purpose: Wales at this time was largely a non-monetary economy, but kings nevertheless were due renders from their people. These could take a variety of forms –consumables, such as bread, dairy products, beer, mead and honey; grain for sowing or milling; animal skins and livestock including pigs, cattle and sheep; services such as building work or military support; and, in some instances, precious metals, either by weight or in the form of coins of Anglo-Saxon or Anglo-Norman origin.[4] Moving from place to place allowed the kings both to collect and consume these renders efficiently, without placing too great a burden upon any one area for too long, or risking that perishable goods might rot before they could be used. While kings may have stayed as guests with members of their nobility from time to time, it is likely that in many cases, the places in which they stayed were their property – royal estates seem to have been scattered throughout each kingdom. This in itself was practical: it helped to maintain the distance between king and subject – wherever he was, he was usually on his own territory, which gave him both practical and psychological advantages. He would be employing his familiar warband as his defenders, rather than leaving his security in the hands of outsiders.

The king's court was known as the *llys*. According to the extant Welsh law codes, this consisted of a number of buildings, including a hall, a sleeping chamber for the royal family, buildings to house domestic activities like cooking and baking, storehouses, shelter for livestock and sleeping quarters for the *teulu* and other members of the household. These would have been fortified in some fashion, presumably by some combination of gates, ditches and palisades. In addition to tax renders, the *llys* was supported by a nearby royal estate, or *maerdref*, worked on behalf of the king by tenants or bondsmen. No certain royal building complexes survive in Wales from the late eleventh century, but we have archaeological evidence of royal strongholds from both earlier and later periods. The hill-forts which may have characterised the royal, aristocratic and other elite inhabitations of the very early medieval period (fifth to seventh centuries) had fallen out of use long before Nest's birth – before, indeed, the rise to power of the royal house of which she was a member.[5] These ancient strongholds bear witness to a relatively wealthy lifestyle. At Dinas Powys, near Cardiff, for instance, archaeological finds included pottery from south-west France and the Mediterranean, suggesting participation in European trade; alongside evidence for metalworking and jewellery making.[6] Its inhabitants, whether royal or aristocratic, lived a comfortable lifestyle, produced surpluses for trade, and were able to support specialised craftsmen. By Nest's time, royal life seems to have been more mobile – and there is less evidence for craft specialisation, perhaps due to the lack of a settled royal centre. We know that a contemporary of her father, Gruffudd ap Llywelyn, king of Gwynedd 1039–1063/4, had a defended stronghold at Rhuddlan,[7] and that one of the latter's successors, Gruffudd ap Cynan, had several major courts within that kingdom.[8] By the mid to later twelfth century, one main hall complex of the kings of Deheubarth lay at Dinefwr, near Llandeilo in Dyfed. Gerald of Wales believed that this had been their main royal seat since ancient times.[9] The castle which now stands there belongs to a later period than that of Nest, but there is some evidence to suggest that Gerald was correct in his belief that a royal centre had existed there before the coming of the Normans to Wales.[10] Another *llys* of the kings of Deheubarth possibly lay at Carreg Cennen.[11] In the *Mabinogion*, Pwyll, the king of Dyfed, has a court at Arberth, and his son and successor Pryderi has another further north at Rhuddlan Teivi in Ceredigion.[12]

What might these *llysoedd* have looked like? A list of buildings as described by the Welsh law codes has been given above. Archaeological excavation in north Wales has revealed the remains of several *llysoedd* in Gwynedd. These date from the thirteenth century, and may thus have been influenced by Anglo-Norman and Angevin styles of building. Nevertheless, at Aber, the foundations of a large stone hall made up of three chambers have been uncovered, which may represent one of the dwellings of the princes of Gwynedd. At Rhosyr, rather more substantial remains have been uncovered, possibly representing the remains of a hall and a separate chamber, while early documentary evidence mentions the presence at the same site also of a chapel and a stable.[13] The hall at Rhosyr may have been mainly constructed of timber, despite its stone foundations,[14] and such a method was probably more common in eleventh-century

Deheubarth. While references to royal *llysoedd* occur in Welsh medieval poetry and prose tales, there are no descriptions of the physical
appearance of these halls. While Norman stone castles served as a
potent symbol of the physical presence – and permanence – of the
Norman invaders, the *llys* of the Welsh king seems to have had a
more social function. It is mentioned in prose and poem as the location for rich feast and celebrations, presided over by an open-handed
king. Hence in the prose tale *Pwyll Pendeuic Dyuet* (Pwyll, Lord of
Dyfed), when the hero Pwyll comes to the court of Heveydd the
Old, whose daughter Rhiannon he seeks to wed:

> There was great joy at their arrival: a huge assembly rejoicing to see
> them and a great feast set out and all the resources of the court placed at
> their disposal. The hall was made ready and they entered and sat down:
> Heveydd sat on one side of Pwyll and Rhiannon on the other, and every-
> one else according to rank. They ate and caroused and conversed ...[15]

Hospitality seems to have been prized not only in a king but in all
householders. Gerald of Wales noted of the Welsh that, 'Everyone's
house is open to all ... When you travel there is no question of your
asking for accommodation or of their offering it: you simply march
into a house and hand over your weapons to the person in charge.'[16]
The guest thus arriving could expect food, bed and entertainment,
and element is again echoed in the prose tales. When in *Culhwch ac
Olwen* the young warrior Culhwch arrives at King Arthur's court,
he is welcomed, well fed and granted the aid of king and court,
even though he has ignored proper custom by riding armed into
the midst of the hall. When Kei questions Arthur's reception of this
young upstart, Arthur replies, 'We are noble men so long as others
come to us, and the more gifts we distribute, the greater will be our
reputation and fame and glory.'[17] Generosity was a valued attribute
not only of kings but also of their wives. The Welsh law codes lay
out at least some of the gift-giving obligations of queens,[18] while
after Pwyll has married Rhiannon and she has come to his court no
visitor leaves without receiving a valuable gift from her.[19] Care must

be observed in applying the testimony of prose tales and law codes. The latter as extant date probably to the later twelfth and thirteenth centuries, and, as far as the king's wife is concerned, may have been influenced by Norman and Angevin practice; in particular to the circumstances attendant upon the intermarriages of the later princes of Gwynedd with illegitimate daughters of Angevin kings.[20] Both law codes and prose tales, moreover, present us with ideal versions of a given situation: the actions of kings and queens are presented in terms of best practice, and this does not necessarily reflect everyday behaviour. Additionally, characters like Arthur or Pwyll or Rhiannon are almost by definition anomalous in terms of daily life. They are not realistic representations of people; they are heroes, whose demeanour and behaviour is expected to differ – sometimes immensely – from the norm. They possess unusual powers or attractions or resources, and they live in courts of unusual richness. Pwyll travels between his own, apparently mundane kingdom, and the supernatural realms both of Rhiannon's father Heveydd and of the underworld king Arawn. Rhiannon possesses almost magical knowledge and powers, and exemplary beauty. Arthur's court is the home of heroes and the fountain of legends. It is unlikely that Rhys ap Tewdwr and his court operated on the scale of opulence imagined in these stories, nor can we be certain that he possessed a formal queen. It is likely, however, that in her father's various houses Nest will have witnessed feasts and gatherings of the leading men of the kingdom, and seen her father (and perhaps her mother) reward favoured or valued supporters with gifts of food, clothing, livestock or ornamentation.

Royal places seem also to have been centres for trade and perhaps craft activity, although this is harder to trace after the early period. As has been mentioned, the elite complex at Dinas Powys was home to metalworkers and jewellers, presumably under the patronage of the lord. The law codes, however, in describing the royal court, do not make much reference to specific crafts: it seems that kings did not reliably support blacksmiths or carpenters or makers of personal ornaments. When another legendary hero, Manawyddan, has to turn to a craft to support himself, he leaves Wales and travels into England in order to find sufficient customers and raw materials.[21] It appears that the needs of the Welsh courts for craftsmen in leather or metal, for example, were insufficient to support a court population of craftspeople.[22] Wendy Davies, indeed, has suggested that many such crafts were carried out on an essentially part-time basis, as part of the regular round of domestic and agrarian work.[23] Probably Rhys ap Tewdwr's household included men and women who could mend a metal pot or make shoes for horses or people, but who also served in other functions, be it cooking or caring for animals or fighting in the warband.

Wales was not a rich country, by the standards of the time, and wealth varied between its kingdoms. Some, such as Nest's native Dyfed and Ystrad Twyi, possessed a reasonable proportion of good agricultural land, particularly in the south and in coastal areas.[24] This provided land suitable for crops of various kinds, particularly grain. Gerald of Wales thought that the main cereal crop was oats,[25] but it is clear from other evidence that other cereals were also cultivated. In *Manawydan uap Lyr*, Manawyddan cultivates wheat at Arberth, and the Welsh law codes refer to land used for the growing of wheat in their account of the food renders due to the king.[26] One of the most famous clauses of Welsh law is that referring to cats — should a cat belonging to the king be killed, the killer had to pay compensation as follows:

> ...her head is set down on a clean level floor, and her tail is raised up, and wheat grains are poured over her until they hide the end of her tail.[27]

The law codes also mention the cultivation of barley and rye,[28] while references to linen clothing suggest the cultivation of flax. Nest's family would have had access to all of these, either through direct cultivation on royal estates or from renders paid to her father. The king often received prepared foodstuffs — bread or beer rather than wheat or oats or barley, but Nest must have become familiar with the various methods of food production, watching the royal cooks or seeing people at work in the fields. Did she play a part in baking and brewing and general cooking? We don't know, but it is likely that she may have had some skills in this area, if only in the preparation of more complex dishes made from rarer ingredients. It may be, however, that cooking was not considered an appropriate activity for women of royal or noble blood. In the prose tale *Branwen uerch Lyr*, it is considered to be a great insult when Branwen is made to cook for the court of her husband, Matholwch.[29] As she grew older, Nest may, however, have sometimes assisted in acquiring food – Rhiannon, at least, accompanies her husband and son to the hunt in *Manawydan*.[30] As the daughter of the king of Deheubarth, Nest probably enjoyed a richer diet than most girls and young women. In addition to good arable land, her father's kingdom had a long coastline, and we know both from archaeology and from written sources that fish and shell-fish were an important food resource. Shellfish and the remains of sea fish were found at Dinas Powys,[31] and Gerald wrote of the value of the long coastline of south-west Wales.[32]

Pastoral farming – and especially cattle breeding – was probably the most significant agricultural activity, and cattle were viewed as a form of wealth in themselves, as well as being a food resource. References to cattle and dairy produce are frequent in Welsh medieval writings, even being mentioned in Chronicle texts.[33] Gerald wrote, '...the entire population lives almost entirely on oats and the produce of their herds, milk, cheese and butter.'[34] Pigs and sheep were also raised, but they seem to have been of lesser importance. Nest probably had little contact with these animals, however, save as a consumer of their produce. The animals she would have known best would be hunting dogs and the horses on which the court travelled. She may also have had pets – the Welsh laws refer to the pet animals of the queen, but do not specify the species. There will certainly have been dogs, but cats – and more particularly kittens – were probably familiar playmates as well.[35]

In the eleventh and twelfth centuries, much of south Wales was forested. Dinefwr itself was surrounded by woodland,[36] while Cantref Mawr, which made up a good half of Ystrad Twyi, was also heavily wooded. These woods were both a resource and a protection. They served to guard the routes to royal sites, provided a home for game animals, including deer, supplied wood for building and heating, and nuts and fruits to add to the diet. Some fruit trees were deliberately planted – Gruffudd ap Cynan, a contemporary of Nest and her father, was said by his later biographer to have encouraged the planting of orchards in his northern kingdom of Gwynedd.[37]

It seems that in most years, Welsh kingdoms produced enough for their own needs, but it is not clear to what extent surpluses could be expected. As has been mentioned, not all parts of Wales were equally productive. Much of Powys, for example, lacked good soils, and for much of the second part of the eleventh century and on into the twelfth, kings and lords from Powys were aggressive and frequent raiders into more productive neighbouring territories. Ceredigion, the long curving land abutting Cardigan Bay, possessed reasonable land and valuable sea resources. It was not securely the possession of any one kingdom, and was the scene of numerous battles, expeditions and conquests. Moreover, while kings possessed estates of their own, they could not maintain themselves without the consent and cooperation of the leading men of their lands. These men – known as *uchelwyr* – were freeborn, land-holding heads of families. They could possess an extensive network of contacts through kinship links, marriage alliances and bonds of fosterage or patronage. Their sons, grandsons, nephews and cousins were the young men who made up the king's *teulu*, warband. They, their families and their tenants, supplied part of the renders in goods and services due to the king. Their support was thus critical to him, and the most powerful amongst them had to be treated with care and respect. Gruffudd ap Cynan, for instance, found it necessary to make tight bonds of marriage with one of the leading families of Gwynedd, that of the sons of Edwin ap Goronwy. These men – brothers Owain and Uchdryd – held important lands in Tegeingl, a key area on the route between Gwynedd and the lands of the Anglo-Norman lords of Chester, and were both ambitious and aggressive. Even marrying their sister Angharad did not secure their support for Gruffudd. In 1098, Owain assisted Hugh, Earl of Chester, in his invasion of Gwynedd, while in the early years of the twelfth century Uchdryd played Gruffudd off against his Welsh neighbours and rivals, the rulers of Powys. As will be discussed below, Rhys ap Tewdwr also had his problems maintaining the support of his *uchelwyr*.

One method of helping to retain support has already been touched upon – generosity. References in Welsh literature from throughout the medieval period urge kings and lords to be generous to their followers and, in particular, to the members of the *teulu*. This generosity could take various forms. One of these was the giving of feasts. The food renders received by the king were expected to be shared, and his warriors were to be both encouraged and rewarded with the best available food and drink. Thus, before their attack upon the Anglo-Saxons, the men of the ancient north British kingdom of Yr Gododdin, '…had been nurtured upon wine and mead.'[38] The dating of this poem is much debated, but its description of the heroism and camaraderie of the warband and the rewards they merited probably reflect what was considered to be the ideal. In its view, warriors who risked their lives for lord and land deserved the best from that lord in return. Food, drink and lodging were not all that were expected: service in the warband might lay the financial foundations for the future of a young man. The law codes lay out regular gifts expected from the king and his wife to specific servants and officers of their courts – clothing of wool and linen was due to much of the household three times a year,[39] a share of plunder from raids was due to various officials,[40] the court bard could expect a harp and a ring upon joining the household,[41] the steward received monetary reward.[42] The Welsh Chronicles are full of accounts of raids, battles and annexations of territory. Many of these had their roots in the rivalries and ambitions of kings, but the warring had economic and social aspects also. Expansion of territory, as was mentioned above, led to increase of resources, and the greater and more productive his lands, the greater the wealth of a king. Kings with greater wealth could attract more supporters and reward them with greater gifts. Activity outside the homeland also served as a distraction: it kept the sons of the *uchelwyr* busy and increased their sense of participation in and belonging to their native kingdom. We know from the Welsh Chronicles that Rhys ap Tewdwr was involved in his share of battles and raids: the young Nest will have grown up familiar with the sight of her father's *teulu* being feasted and rewarded before and after battles. She must have watched them arm and ride or march out, and she will, too, have seen them return. The sight cannot always have been pleasant, as men returned injured and bloody. When captives were taken – and eleventh-century Wales was a slave-owning culture – their condition may have been pitiable. Nest will have been brought up to consider all this normal, and to deal with both the positive and negative side-effects of war.

Although Wales had been part of the Roman Empire, much of it had been under military, rather than civilian, control and towns had not really developed. The mobility of the kings probably contributed to this: no one *llys* became important enough, at least before the thirteenth century, to encourage the development around it of a settlement of any considerable size. Geography also favoured dispersed settlement, as, particularly in upland areas, the available land resources could not support more than a small number of people. Most of the population lived in scattered farms and crofts, from which they produced enough to support themselves. Not all of the population was free: bondsmen worked the land of the king and the nobility, and their labour would have helped to support their masters as well as themselves, with a small surplus, at least in some years. But there were no markets as such – these were to be introduced under the Anglo-Normans. This is not to say that there was no trade. Trading activities certainly occurred. Travelling craftsmen brought their skills and wares to the courts, to the houses of the nobility and to the larger churches.[43] We know too that by the tenth century there was a small Viking staging post and perhaps trade centre on Anglesey,[44] and place name evidence reveals that the Vikings knew and sailed the south Welsh coast also. Rhys ap Tewdwr had dealings with Vikings from Ireland as mercenaries, and it is likely that their trading counterparts also visited his lands. Welsh documentary evidence treats the Vikings as raiders and warriors, but this was by no means their only activity within the Irish Sea area. The Vikings were amongst the greatest traders of the early Middle Ages. Their ships and merchants travelled almost the length and breadth of the known world, from the Black Sea and Byzantium in the east to the fringes of Newfoundland, from modern Lappland to the shores of North Africa. Evidence for the sorts of items they brought into and from Wales is limited, but we know from excavations and written material elsewhere that they traded in amber, furs, timber, silver and gold, slaves, falcons, soapstone, and silk.[45] Dublin, Wexford, Waterford, Cork and Limerick in Ireland were all Scandinavian settlements and trade centres, and Wales lay within their ambit. Rhys himself not only hired Vikings as mercenaries but retreated to Ireland – most probably to Dublin – for a short time when under pressure from Welsh neighbours. His contemporary Gruffudd ap Cynan of Gwynedd had an Irish-Scandinavian princess as his mother and maintained close links to her home town of Dublin. Viking traders certainly came to coastal south Wales – to the monasteries of St Davids and Llancarfan, and what are now Swansea, Milford Haven and perhaps elsewhere. We do not know if they were allowed to travel inland to Rhys' court (it is likely they were not: Vikings were opportunists and some of the slaves they traded had been seized in raids on Wales) or whether he met with them or their agents on the coast. But Nest will have seen their goods brought to her father and his household for inspection, and perhaps she may have watched their long-ships under sail along the Welsh coast, and wondered whether they came on a peaceful or an aggressive mission. These travellers, when not bent on raiding, would have brought with them not only trade goods, but news from Scandinavia and Ireland, Scotland, the Northern and Western Isles, the Isle of Man, France and perhaps even the Mediterranean. When Nest's father resorted to employing mercenaries from the Viking settlements in Ireland in 1088, she may have seen them gathered in the hall alongside the regular *teulu*, and listened to them talking in Irish or Old Norse.[46]

Communication outside Wales was not restricted to the Scandinavians settled in Ireland. We know that Rhys had contacts with the new Norman rulers of England, a point which will be expanded upon later. His territorial interests expanded quite a long way eastwards, and seem to have included the area around Brecon, close to the border with England. The population of the border shires – Gloucestershire, Herefordshire, Shropshire and Cheshire – included people of Welsh origin. Indeed, Rhys' kinsmen Maredudd ab Owain and Gruffudd ap Maredudd held lands in Herefordshire, granted to them originally by its first Norman earl, William fitz Osbern.[47] There is evidence pointing to the existence of individuals who were fluent both in English (or Norman French) and Welsh and who acted as translators.[48] It is highly likely that such translators existed well before the Norman conquest and the growth of Norman 'marcher' lordships along the Welsh border. In the 1050s an Anglo-Saxon earl, Aelfgar, allied himself with the then king of Gwynedd, Gruffudd ap Llywelyn: the two must have had a spoken means of communication.[49] There will have been trade across the border, and discussions of land rights. English craftsmen may have visited Rhys' court with their wares, and he must have had at least some dealings with Anglo-Norman officials from the border shires. It is very likely that Rhys' household included at least one person who spoke English, and perhaps someone with at least some knowledge of French. As an adult Nest herself must have been bilingual in Welsh and French, although we cannot assume that she learnt any language other than Welsh while in her father's court.

There was also communication between religious houses. The Welsh churches had a lively tradition of travel and foreign contacts, especially with Ireland and with Brittany, although the volume of this had probably decreased since the rise of Viking raiders from the ninth century onwards. Welsh monks compiling chronicles of their own country had access to Irish chronicle texts.[50] Sulien, bishop of St Davids 1072/3–1078 and again 1085–1088 travelled to and studied in churches in Ireland and perhaps Scotland in his youth (and may, indeed, have assisted Rhys, in whose lands his bishopric lay, in communicating with the Hiberno-Scandinavians).[51] Monks and priests from Ireland visited Wales, and may perhaps have come to Rhys' court. St Davids probably also had some contact with churches in England, notably Canterbury, Hereford and perhaps Worcester. Perhaps St Davids also maintained some contact with Brittany: we do not know. Wales in the years of Nest's childhood lay to one side of the European mainstream, certainly, but it was not isolated, and her father's court will have known of events in England, Normandy, Scandinavia and Ireland.

Late eleventh-century Wales was a securely Christian country. Christianity had been introduced under the Romans, and seems to have been widely adopted throughout Wales by the time of the Anglo-Saxon historian Bede, who wrote in the early eighth century. His *Ecclesiastical History* tells us of bishops and monks from Wales.[52] One of his sources was the British monk Gildas, who wrote probably in the mid-sixth century, during the period of the Anglo-Saxon settlement of England. He too records bishops and monks of the Britons (the predecessors of the Welsh) and bewails the unchristian behaviour of some of their kings.[53] The churches of eleventh-century Wales differed in organisation and form from those found in England and on the continent, and the Norman invaders were rather shocked by them. Priests and bishops were not required to be celibate,[54] and the sons of priests often became priests or monks themselves.[55] Monasteries, likewise, could be family concerns, rather than celibate communities, and their communities were hereditary, operating in some ways more like small villages than a conventional monastic community. There seems to have been no tradition of women entering the church as nuns. But there is no evidence to suggest a lack of faith amongst the Welsh and in general people were professed Christians.[56] Nest's name reflects this: it is a Welsh form of Agnes, referencing not only the saint of that name, but also the idea of Christ as the Lamb, *agnus,* of God. It was by no means an uncommon name at the time: we know of at least one other Nest, also born of a Welsh royal line – this was Nest daughter of Gruffudd ap Llywelyn (died *c.* 1064) who married Osbern fitz Richard, lord of Richard's Castle in Herefordshire.[57] Nest ferch Gruffudd named her own daughter Nest, and our Nest's brother Gruffudd ap Rhys also had a daughter of this name. It stands out, somewhat, amongst the other female names known to have been in use amongst Welsh royal lines in the later eleventh and early twelfth centuries, in its religious connotations. Otherwise at this period we hear of women named Angharad and Gwenllian. Angharad means 'much loved' and belongs to the category of female names with connotations of affection or cherishing;[58] Gwenllian derives from the words for white, fair and flaxen, and probably originally referred to hair colour.[59] Perhaps either Rhys or his wife Gwladus ferch Rhiwallon, were religious.[60]

HER ANCESTRY: THE KINGS OF DEHEUBARTH

Nest was born into one of the most important of the Welsh royal families, the southern branch of the Line of Merfyn.[61] This ancestry was probably important to her – certainly, the genealogy of this family and its northern cousins was known to her grandson Gerald, who cites their pedigrees in his *Description of Wales*.[62] It is likely he learnt it from his mother Angharad, Nest's daughter. In twelfth-century Welsh terms, his descent – and Nest's – was highly distinguished and worth mentioning: they were the kinsmen of two of the three major native rulers and descendants of the great names of the past.

As far as we know, this family had first come to power in the first quarter of the ninth century, not in Dyfed, but in the northern kingdom, Gwynedd. The origins of this line are uncertain:[63] what we do know is that in around 825, Gwynedd came into the power of one Merfyn Frych ap Gwriad. He was not a member of the preceding ruling family. We do not know if he had any connexion with any of the leading families of Gwynedd at that time, nor does it seem that his descendants preserved any tale of his origins. Pedigrees compiled long after his death hint that he may have been descended from one of the ancient ruling families of the old Welsh kingdoms which once flourished in north Britain (in what is now Cumbria and Strathclyde). But it seems that no-one was sure. His nickname – *frych*, freckled – is perhaps a clue as to what he looked like, and a suggestion that his degree of freckled-ness was notable. We know he died in 844. Apart from this, we know one other thing: he was to found a dynasty which would survive right down to the eclipse of independent Wales in 1283.

His son is known to history as Rhodri Mawr, Rhodri the Great. While Merfyn probably restricted his activities to Gwynedd, Rhodri was more ambitious. He expanded his control eastwards into Powys and southwards into Ceredigion. This policy of aggression was continued by his sons Anarawd and Cadell after his death in battle 878. By 904, Cadell ap Rhodri had displaced the last member of the old royal line of Dyfed and installed himself there. His control was sufficiently strong that, on his death in 910 no scion of the old line survived to mount a challenge, and Cadell's son Hywel succeeded to his lands and power.

Hywel ap Cadell may have been one of the ancestors of whom Nest was most proud, and under the more familiar name Hywel Dda, Hywel the Good, he remains one of the best known of all the Welsh kings. Citing the pedigree of the kings of Deheubarth, Gerald makes an especial point of mentioning Hywel, taking care to translate his nickname, which he does not do for Rhodri Mawr. By the twelfth century, Hywel was a notable figure, considered to be the father of native Welsh law and a symbol of good rulership. It was certainly to Hywel that Nest's father Rhys owed the foundations of his own kingdom: although Cadell had spearheaded the movement south, it was Hywel who consolidated them. He secured his control over both Dyfed and Ystrad Twyi, repulsing the ambitions of his northern cousins and he expanded his influence to the south-east, bringing Morgannwg under his overlordship, if not his direct control. He also entered into some form of relationship with his Anglo-Saxon neighbours, attending the courts of kings Athelstan and Eadred. This relationship was probably partly alliance, partly submission: friendship with the Anglo-Saxon kings helped Hywel against the Viking raiders and colonists who were active throughout the British Isles in the tenth century, and Athelstan may also have assisted him against his rival kinsmen from Gwynedd. The relationship certainly added to the security of Hywel's kingship. It was to have long-term effects which were less desirable, leading to an apparent belief by the Anglo-Norman kings (and perhaps some of their Anglo-Saxon predecessors) in a right to overlordship over Wales, but in contemporary tenth-century terms, it was a sensible move.[64] The memory he left in Wales seems to have been a good one: his image is that of a wise, pious and just king.[65]

The promulgation of the legend of Hywel probably began with his son and successor Owain,[66] who may have been responsible for the compilation of our earliest surviving Welsh pedigrees and Chronicle text.[67] During his long reign (*c*.950–988), the Line of Merfyn flourished in south Wales and his two effective and active sons, Einion and Maredudd, assisted him in advancing control over the south-east and in expanding northwards through Ceredigion and into Gwynedd.[68] They were successful, but their ambitions perhaps did not always make them popular. A warning note was struck in 984 when the *uchelwyr*, the leading men, of Gwent in the south-east fell upon Einion and killed him. His brother Maredudd, who was probably the younger of the two, went on to achieve a wide hegemony, influencing and perhaps controlling not only most of south Wales but the entirety of the north as well. His dominion over south-central Wales and the border territories of Buellt and Brycheiniog was built upon his brother's successes of the 970s and early 980s, but the northwards expansion occurred on his own initiative, subsequent to the deaths of his brother and father, and during the late 980s and early 990s, he achieved virtual control over all Wales.

Of the two brothers, Maredudd was undeniably the most successful, but his legacy was short-lived, and he was not to occupy a particularly large place in later Welsh historiography.[69] He was king in his own right, whereas Einion predeceased their father and may never have been considered as a king.[70] There are several reasons for the relative obscurity of Maredudd. In the first instance, he failed to leave successful male heirs. He is recalled mainly in pedigrees relating to the kingdom of Powys, whose rulers in the eleventh, twelfth and thirteenth centuries claimed descent from his daughter Angharad.

Later rulers in Deheubarth had no need to recall his memory, and may indeed have seen his descendants more as rivals than anything else. Furthermore, Maredudd's achievements were to be short-lived. His ambitions in the north were to be fulfilled only short-term. The native ruling house of Gwynedd, the northern branch of the Line of Merfyn, had splintered into a variety of factions, each representing different groups of descendants of Rhodri Mawr, and warfare between them was frequent. While Maredudd was able to exploit this, he did not succeed in destroying the factions, nor, given the regularity with which new claimants to the kingship of Gwynedd appeared, did he manage to secure for himself the allegiance of that kingdom's leading men. Towards the end of his reign, his position in the south came under threat from his nephew, Edwin ab Einion who may have had English backing.[71]

Edwin is said in the pedigrees to have had three brothers: Cadell, Goronwy and Tewdwr. The first two are obscure: we are slightly better informed about Tewdwr. Unlike Edwin, Tewdwr supported Maredudd. We know very little about him, other than that he was killed in 993 assisting Maredudd. This is interesting for a number of reasons. Succession to kingships in early Wales was by no means restricted to sons of a ruling king – any male relative who was descended in the male line from a king was in theory eligible, and kings might be succeeded by brothers, cousins, nephews or uncles as well as sons.[72] These relatives did not – before the thirteenth century, at least – have to be legitimate. Maredudd had at least one son, Cadwallon, who had died in 992. It may have been the latter's death which prompted Edwin's invasion: the death of a son who may have been the recognised heir created a vacuum which Edwin was anxious to fill.[73] Edwin too probably died in 992, killed in his own invasion. Tewdwr was likely to be Maredudd's closest surviving male relative and may well have stepped forward into the position of heir. His support of Maredudd in the following year is thus explicable. In the end, it was to give him no benefit, as he predeceased his uncle.

Maredudd died in 999, and the events which followed are unclear. We do not know the name of his successor or successors: all we know

for certain is that the southern branch of the Line of Merfyn survived in Deheubarth through the sons and grandsons of Maredudd's
brother Einion. The apparent uncertainty of Maredudd's last years
and those immediately following is partly a result of a lack of records
(our extant chronicles are thin for this period). But it was also a
consequence of the nature of the medieval Welsh political system:
as has been mentioned, inheritance from father to eldest son – or,
indeed to any son – was not an established practice, and it could take
a gap of several generations before a line descended from a king via
an unsuccessful son was completely excluded from at least a right to
try for the kingship.[74] Nor did kings necessarily rule alone: it is not
unprecedented for groups of brothers to share power. Sometimes
they might also make a territorial division, but this did not always
happen, and brothers in particular might sometimes share territory.
This arrangement, however, tended to break down once the kinship
bounds became more distant, and it is rare to find uncle and nephew
or groups of cousins co-ruling peacefully. Under the influence of
Anglo-Norman practice and expectations, this system broke down
during the later twelfth and thirteenth centuries, but in the lifetime
of Nest's great-grandfather, Cadell ab Einion, and his son Tewdwr
ap Cadell, it was still in operation. We have no strong evidence, but
subsequent upon Maredudd's death, his territories in Deheubarth
probably broke up and passed into the control of a mixture of his
male kinsmen. He had already lost control over the north before his
death: it is likely that the south-eastern territories also returned to
the hands of native royal or aristocratic lines.

WALES IN THE ELEVENTH CENTURY

For the first twenty or so years of the eleventh century, it seems that
no one man achieved a strong power base either within or across
any of the Welsh kingdoms. Nest's family, the Line of Merfyn, was
temporarily in eclipse. The years between about 1020 and 1065 were
to see the rise of three new royal lines. In the end, only one of these

would survive to become a major player in Welsh political life on into the twelfth and thirteenth centuries, but the effects of all three were to be marked. The first was the line of Llywelyn ap Seisyll. Their ancestry is completely obscure: we do not even know from which part of Wales they came. But by 1022, Llywelyn was securely king of Gwynedd, and had influence, if not direct control, over Deheubarth. When the latter was invaded from Ireland, it was Llywelyn who came to repel the invaders. The latter were lead by one Rhain, who claimed to be a son of Maredudd ab Owain: Llywelyn routed him, then plundered Deheubarth. It is entirely possible that he already had control over at least parts of that kingdom before Rhain's invasion, and that the latter may have been acting with the collusion of some of the native nobility: Llywelyn's ravaging of the land may have been as much punishment as warning. He died the following year, but the effects of his family upon Wales were only just beginning.[75]

The second of the new families was that of Rhydderch ab Iestyn.[76] This line came from Gwent, one of the constituents of the south-eastern kingdom of Morgannwg. The family was probably from the class of *uchelwyr*, leading men, and was to survive at least as local magnates into the thirteenth century. Rhydderch was the first of this line to make a recorded impression upon Welsh political life. Llywelyn ap Seisyll seems to have created or caused considerable disarray amongst the descendants of the Line of Merfyn, both in Gwynedd and in Deheubarth, and Rhydderch stepped into the vacuum left by his death. He must already have been king in Morgannwg. In 1023 he annexed Deheubarth, and held it until his death ten years later in 1033. Our sources are silent as to whether he had any designs on the north. But whoever held power in Gwynedd and Powys, it seems they offered him no threat in the south. His death led to a brief resurgence of the Line of Merfyn within Deheubarth, in the person of Hywel ab Edwin ab Einion, who was Nest's grandfather's cousin.[77] Hywel proved to be a competent and effective king, retaining power for around a decade. At another time, he might have continued as king, passing on his lands to a son or nephew, and creating a southern branch of the Line of Merfyn which would have by-passed Rhys ap Tewdwr. But Hywel was to come up against a major challenge, in the form of Gruffudd ap Llywelyn, perhaps the most extraordinary ruler Wales was ever to know, and one who would change its political life forever.

Gruffudd was the son of Llywelyn ap Seisyll by his wife, Angharad, daughter of the former king of Deheubarth, Maredudd ab Owain. He was thus kin on his mother's side to the Line of Merfyn, but in mid-eleventh-century Wales, this did not count for much. Women could not pass on any claim on the lands or powers of their birth families to their sons. In 1039, Gruffudd made himself king of Gwynedd, and immediately turned his eyes southwards. From the very beginning of his reign, he was a king bound on conquest: perhaps the most aggressive and determined Welsh leader since Rhodri Mawr. He harassed and harried Hywel ab Edwin throughout the next five years, eventually succeeding in killing him in 1044. He seemingly already held Powys, and had designs on the south-east. His expansion was to be blocked for another decade by Gruffudd ap Rhydderch ab Iestyn, himself a gifted and effective leader. Gruffudd ap Rhydderch proved himself a worthy successor to Rhydderch ab Iestyn, dominating Morgannwg and vying forcefully with Gruffudd ap Llywelyn for control of Deheubarth.[78] He seems to have followed in his father's tracks during the earlier 1050s, keeping Gruffudd ap Llywelyn out of most of the south. But in 1055 or 1056 Gruffudd ap Rhydderch also fell victim to the ambitious king of Gwynedd. His death left no rivals to Gruffudd ap Llywelyn anywhere in Wales, and he was to rule the whole country – the first and only man to do so – until his death in 1063–4.

Gruffudd ap Llywelyn's influence was not confined to Wales: alongside his aggression towards his Welsh neighbours, he pursued a strong policy regarding the long border with England. He launched a number of raids into England in the 1040s and 1050s, but his concerns were with more than just plunder or small amounts of territorial expansion. As long ago as the ninth century, kings of Anglo-Saxon England had involved themselves in the internal politics of Wales.[79] Gruffudd chose to intervene in the internal affairs of England. He formed an alliance with Earl Aelfgar, a leading member of the court of King Edward the Confessor, and the two of them formed a potent faction against the ambition of Earl Harold Godwinesson, brother of Edward's queen and one of the most powerful men in England. As a result, Gruffudd was able to expand his territory in the Welsh borders without reprisals and without fear of English invasion. To seal his alliance, he married Aelfgar's daughter Ealdgyth. Aelfgar, in turn, was able to resist Harold's attempts to erode his lands and influence. But although their relationship served both men well through the 1050s, it was to have long-reaching consequences, and helped lay the foundations for the Norman attitude to the Welsh and their leaders. The death of Aelfgar — whose sons seem to have inherited his alliance but were still under-age — left Gruffudd exposed, and after a major invasion of his lands by Earl Harold, he was murdered, probably by his own household, in late 1063 or 1064.[80]

Gruffudd ap Llywelyn left a deep impression on Wales: a century after his death, folk-tales about him were circulating in the borders to be recorded by the Anglo-Welsh writer Walter Map.[81] The compilers of the Welsh Chronicles remembered him as a great warrior against the English and the Hiberno-Scandinavians and, at his death, described him as 'head and shield and defender to the Britons'.[82] The biographer of Gruffudd ap Cynan cited him as the predecessor to whose powers the younger Gruffudd should aspire.[83] His eight years as king of all Wales was unprecedented: not even Hywel Dda or Maredudd ab Owain had achieved such wide or such lasting control. His reign became a benchmark for the ambitions of later kings, and in particular for kings from Gwynedd. Though he died before Nest's birth, her father Rhys may have seen him as he travelled from *llys* to *llys*. Could Rhys have served in Gruffudd's warband or at least in one of his wider armies? Rhys cannot have been a particularly young man when he became king of Deheubarth in 1079. Later tradition held that Gruffudd was suspicious of young men of good family or with skill at arms, and at least one young dynast was brought up in Ireland, out of his reach.[84] In adulthood, Rhys had dealings with the Vikings settled in Ireland and it is not impossible that he spent some of his youth amongst them.[85] We can identify a few members of Gruffudd's *teulu* with reasonable confidence – his two half-brothers Bleddyn and Rhiwallon, his sons Maredudd and Ithel, and perhaps one Trahaearn ap Caradog, a distant relative by marriage. All of these were from north or north-central Wales. Rhys ap Tewdwr, as a member of the old southern branch of the Line of Merfyn, was more likely to be viewed as a rival, not a potential supporter. The rivalry between north and south – and especially between Deheubarth and Gwynedd – had been a keynote of Welsh politics in the later tenth and eleventh centuries and would continue to be so during the twelfth. Rhys and his court must have remembered Gruffudd ap Llywelyn with a mixture of resentment and respect, and to Nest he may have been an intimidating tradition.

He left a fearsome memory behind him in the Welsh borders, and the consequences of that were to be particularly damaging for Wales. He died less than three years before the Norman Conquest of England: his deeds were still fresh. Those border landholders who survived the Conquest and who formed relations with the new king, William the Conqueror, will have told warning tales of the dangers of allowing a powerful king to rule in Wales. William was alert to the dangers of unreliable neighbours, as he had long had them in his duchy of Normandy. He would not have looked favourably upon an alliance between one of his men and an independent Welsh leader. When Earl Aelfgar's sons, Edwin and Morcar, turned to Gruffudd's half-brother and successor Bleddyn for aid against William, the latter reacted sternly. Rhys ap Tewdwr did not inherit Gruffudd's wide hegemony, but he was to find himself facing the consequences of Gruffudd's foreign policy.

A further result of the reign of Gruffudd ap Llywelyn came out of the succession to him. On his death, his dominion broke apart, and Deheubarth returned into the hands of the southern branch of the Line of Merfyn. Its new lords were Hywel, Maredudd and Rhys, sons of Owain ap Edwin. They were Rhys' cousins and it is quite possible that he served under them as ally and warrior. While Gruffudd ap Llywelyn lived, it would have been difficult, if not

impossible, for Rhys to begin to build himself a network of friendship and alliance in the south. His kinsmen would not have looked
favourably, either, had he made any such attempt to garner support
openly, but he may at least have been in a position to familiarise
himself with the leading men of Deheubarth. While the sons of
Owain consolidated their shared rule in the south, Gwynedd and
Powys passed into the hands of Gruffudd's half-brothers, Bleddyn
and Rhiwallon sons of Cynfyn. The heartland of these brothers was
Powys: it is likely that their father, Angharad ferch Maredudd's second husband Cynfyn ap Gwerystan, was one of the *uchelwyr* of that
kingdom. Bleddyn was to rule in north Wales until 1075, and after his
death was remembered as 'the most beloved and the most merciful
of all kings … a defence for the weak and the strength of the learned
and the honour of the churches and the foundation and comfort of
the lands … '[86] Between 1064 and 1075 he certainly ruled Powys and
Gwynedd, and very probably Ceredigion.[87] Nor had he forgotten
his half-brother's wider hegemony: he was killed in 1075 fighting
in Ystrad Tywi. Bleddyn's career and memory were to have serious
consequences for Rhys ap Tewdwr: Bleddyn's successor, his cousin
Trahaearn ap Caradog, carried a serious grudge against the men of
Deheubarth and its rulers, over which he was more than willing to
go to war. And then, Bleddyn left sons. The lives of both Rhys and
Nest were to be seriously affected by the activities of the family of
Bleddyn.

This dynasty – the Line of Bleddyn – became the new ruling
house of Powys, and was to be the sole native royal line to survive
the conquest of Wales by Edward I in 1283 still in control of their
heartland. The great Owain Glyndŵr, who resurrected the cause of
Welsh independence in the late fourteenth and early fifteenth centuries, was a direct descendant of Bleddyn ap Cynfyn. The family
was to prove the most successful of the three new lines which arose
during the dynamic years of the eleventh century.

Alongside these developments in the internal politics of Wales,
Rhys ap Tewdwr was witness to the arrival in the British Isles of an
entirely new force – the Normans. Unlike Bleddyn ap Cynfyn, who

assisted the Anglo-Saxon Earl Edwin of Mercia against the new conquerors in the 1060s,[88] Rhys probably had had little direct contact
with this new neighbour in the first years of their conquest. But, as
has already been mentioned, their actions and their beliefs about the
Welsh would be matters he could neither ignore nor overcome.

HER FATHER, RHYS AP TEWDWR

What do we know about Rhys? He first appears in our records in
1079, when the Welsh Chronicles record his accession to power. He
was, as we have seen, a member of the southern branch of the Line
of Merfyn, and cousin to the previous kings of Deheubarth, Rhys
and Hywel, sons of Owain. All three were descendents of Einion ab
Owain, the aggressive and ambitious grandson of Hywel Dda who
was killed in Gower in 988. We cannot be certain that either the
father, Tewdwr ap Cadell or the grandfather, Cadell ap Einion, of
Rhys ap Tewdwr were ever kings themselves. They are not noted in
any early Welsh record save for pedigrees, and in those they appear
simply as ancestors. Apart from the fact that they had children, we
know nothing about them (as had been mentioned, our historical records are thin for the period *c.*999 to *c.*1020). This does not
mean that they were necessarily powerless. One of Cadell's brothers, Edwin, had challenged Maredudd ab Owain ap Hywel Dda for
control of Deheubarth in 992, and another, Tewdwr, was killed in
994 supporting Maredudd in the north. It is likely that Cadell was
active alongside his brothers, perhaps in alliance with Edwin against
Maredudd, perhaps fighting in Maredudd's warband. He would have
known the leading men of Deheubarth, and after Maredudd's death
he may have acquired some power over at least part of that kingdom.
Similarly, his son may have ruled over at least some part of the south-
west. We might be sensible, however, to imagine their position as
tenuous or weak, in the face of the aggressive and effective Llywelyn
ap Seisyll and Rhydderch ap Iestyn. In 1022, as has been mentioned,
Deheubarth was invaded by one Rhain, who claimed to be a son of

Maredudd ab Owain. His incursion was met by Llywelyn ap Seisyll, not Cadell or Tewdwr. The immediate ancestors of Rhys ap Tewdwr were insecure in any power they held.

We do not know when Rhys was born. Cadell's brothers were active in the 990s, at which point they were probably in their 20s (their father had died in 984, which gives us a latest possible birth date for Cadell). It is possible that he may have been nominal king in Deheubarth – or perhaps only Dyfed – between 999 and around 1022, in which year he could have been aged *c.*40–60. It might be that it was his death which prompted Rhain's invasion; perhaps faced with the threat of Llywelyn on their northern borders, the leading men of Deheubarth turned to this dubious claimant as an alternative. Tewdwr, however, seems never to have been a sole king.[89] Llywelyn apparently dominated the south until 1023 and Rhydderch ab Iestyn from Morgannwg followed him. But on the latter's death in 1033, the new kings of Deheubarth were Hywel and Maredudd sons of Edwin ab Einion.

They cannot have been very young men: their father Edwin disappears from our records in 992, and by 1033 his sons were probably in their late 30s or 40s. They were competent, experienced and effective, first driving out the sons of Rhydderch and then repelling the sons of Cynan ap Seisyll from the north.[90] As it appears that Rhys ap Tewdwr was an experienced warrior when he became king, it is possible he served in the *teulu* of his cousins. If so, he would not have, however, been the *penteulu*. Not only would he have been far too young, but more importantly Hywel and Maredudd had another brother, Owain. Owain does not seem to have been associated with them in the kingship. It has been plausibly suggested that in some instances the position of *penteulu* may have been awarded to a kinsman who had chosen to exempt himself from any claim to the kingship.[91] Under Hywel and Maredudd, Owain probably held this office. But Rhys ap Tewdwr, as a kinsman, could have been one of the household warriors, perhaps alongside his father Tewdwr. He may not have been very old as, according to the Welsh Laws, a boy became eligible for entry into the *teulu* at the age of fourteen.

Service under Hywel ab Edwin must have provided a useful, if sometimes dangerous, apprenticeship.[92] Hywel was an effective leader, but he had the misfortune to be contemporary to the great Gruffudd ap Llywelyn. From 1039, until his death in battle in 1044, he faced almost continuous aggression from his ambitious northern neighbour. Besides this, his coastline was harassed by Vikings from Ireland in the early 1040s and he may have been under pressure to the east also, where Gruffudd ap Rhydderch ab Iestyn was rising to power over Morgannwg. Rhys ap Tewdwr must have had plenty of experience of battle against both native and foreign enemies.

Hywel's dealings with the Vikings of Ireland were more than simply hostile. Although he successfully expelled them from his lands in 1042, the following year he was himself driven out of Deheubarth by Gruffudd ap Llywelyn and fled to Ireland. There, he hired a Viking mercenary fleet to assist in an attempt to reinstate himself. The attempt failed, but this connexion to Ireland may have been important to Rhys. As was noted earlier, Gruffudd had a reputation of being actively hostile to any potential rival. Remaining in Wales after the death of his royal kinsman would have been dangerous for Rhys. It may be that he took refuge in Ireland with his kinsman's former allies to escape the threat of Gruffudd. If so, he was probably accompanied by other relatives, in particular Hywel's nephews, the sons of Owain ab Edwin. We might imagine the four young men – some of them still perhaps children – forming close bonds with each other while exiled amongst strangers who did not speak their native tongue.

It must be emphasised that this is speculation: we have no hard-and-fast evidence as to the doings of Rhys or his cousins in the 1050s and 1060s. They only appear in our records from 1075, and it may be that all of them were small children – or not even born – when Hywel ab Edwin fell in 1044. Some aspects of the later career of Rhys ap Tewdwr – and, indeed in that of his son Gruffudd – make more sense if we postulate such a period of exile in Ireland, however. He seems to have lacked very close ties to the *uchelwyr* of Deheubarth, and was unable to be certain in all circumstances of their loyalty.

There are various possible explanations for this. His section of the royal house of Deheubarth was at least one and perhaps three generations removed from kingship, and as such he may have been considered an outside candidate. Certainly, he was obliged to wait while his cousins, the sons of Owain ab Edwin, reigned. As nephews of Hywel ab Edwin, they were more clearly close to a known and remembered king, and thus more likely to gain the support of the leading men, even if they had spent part of their youth in exile. An exile without close links to a former king would have seemed less appealing and may have had fewer opportunities to build relationships with the *uchelwyr*. If Rhys had spent a number of years in Ireland, he may have appeared very much an unknown quantity.[93] The *uchelwyr* may have hesitated to trust him. It is, of course, also possible that he lacked personal skills, or was rather uncharismatic.

If Rhys and his cousins had been in exile, they probably returned to Wales after the death in 1063/4 of Gruffudd ap Llywelyn. The fall of the latter must have presented an attractive opportunity, but it was to take over a decade before the cousins could fully exploit it. Gruffudd was gone, but Bleddyn ap Cynfyn was alive and active, while in the south-east, one Caradog ap Gruffudd made himself pre-eminent. Caradog was another descendant of Rhydderch ab Iestyn – the son of his gifted son Gruffudd – and was himself a remarkable man. He is our first recorded Welsh ruler to form a relationship with the new neighbours, the Normans. In 1072, he made an alliance with his new neighbour, Roger de Breteuil, the earl of Hereford, to attack Maredudd ab Owain ab Edwin, one of the three brothers holding Deheubarth. It proved a success: Maredudd lost his life. But Caradog's attitude to the Normans seems by and large to have mirrored the approach taken by other Welsh rulers to neighbours, be they Anglo-Saxon or Viking – a force on the border to be resisted or exploited as circumstances warranted.[94] Caradog's main ally was not the earl of Hereford but the king of Gwynedd and Powys from 1075, Trahaearn ap Caradog, and together the two dominated Wales during the second half of the 1070s. These were the rivals faced by Rhys and his cousins, and they were not to be discounted lightly. The sons of Owain certainly possessed a hereditary claim to rule Deheubarth, but Caradog and Trahaearn were not willing to relinquish their own ambitions and influence. Their hostility to the sons of Owain was compounded by what may have been a personal enmity between Rhys and Trahaearn. In 1075, Bleddyn ap Cynfyn was killed in Ystrad Tywi. All our Welsh Chronicles add that Rhys ab Owain was the man who killed him, and imply that the encounter was itself the result of treachery. Did Rhys ambush Bleddyn, or invite him to a meeting and then turn on him? We do not know, and we must be careful in accepting the word of the Chronicles uncritically. For this period, and for some years further down into the twelfth century, the compiler of the Chronicles betrays considerable pro-Powys sympathies, and his account of Rhys is probably contaminated by this.[95] Whatever the truth, however, Trahaearn appears to have pursued an active policy of revenge against Rhys, and his ally Caradog ap Gruffudd joined him in this, as did some of the *uchelwyr* of Powys. Between 1075 and 1078, Rhys ab Owain faced continuous aggression from both his northern and eastern neighbours, fighting battles on an annual basis and probably unable to spend the time he needed to secure his position within Deheubarth. He and his remaining brother Hywel were killed in 1078 in battle with Caradog ap Gruffudd, having already been routed by Trahaearn.

Rhys ap Tewdwr very probably served alongside his cousins in these turbulent years, and if the account of the Chronicles can be trusted, was lucky to survive.[96] If he had not already fought under Hywel ab Edwin in the 1040s, he must now have gained considerable battle experience. As a close kinsman of the rulers of Deheubarth, he would have rapidly become familiar with all its leading men: his colleagues in the *teulu* were their sons, grandsons, nephews and brothers. The fighting must have left him with strong impressions of the abilities – and perhaps the charisma – of Trahaearn and Caradog. The deaths of Rhys and Hywel sons of Owain left him the next acceptable claimant to Deheubarth from the Line of Merfyn. In 1078, this was not an enviable position. His family had been in eclipse in the south since the death of Hywel ab Edwin in 1044, and his three cous-

ins, Maredudd, Rhys and Hywel, had hung on for only a handful of
years before meeting violent ends. The kingship of Deheubarth may
have looked to him like a poisoned chalice. But, in the following
year, 1079, he was declared king.

By 1079, he may not have been a young man. Our lack of information about his father and grandfather makes it hard to guess even
roughly when he was born. His great-grandfather Einion ab Owain
was active 970 to 984. We cannot know when he fathered Cadell, but
the latter cannot have been younger than sixteen – and was probably
older – by the year 1000, and probably fathered his own son Tewdwr
in the early years of the eleventh century.[97] Rhys was probably born
at some point between 1020 and 1045, although it must be emphasised that this is speculation. In 1079, he was probably somewhere
between about 30 and about 50 years old.

Was Nest born before her father became king? We do not know.
Perhaps we might imagine her as a very young child living on her
father's estate in an atmosphere of danger and continuous warfare. It
is more likely, however, that neither Nest nor her brother Gruffudd
were born by 1079. The reasons for this will be examined later.

The accession to power of Rhys did not put an end to the war in
south Wales, but the death of Rhys ab Owain did produce a breathing
space. Having encompassed the death of his rival, Trahaearn retired
back into Gwynedd. His aggression seems to have been more personal than fuelled by any ambition to seize any part of Deheubarth.
He had other distractions: in 1075, his lands in Gwynedd had been
harassed by a new claimant to kingship, Gruffudd ap Cynan, and he
may have needed to reinforce his control, particularly in western
areas. He faced pressure to the east, also, from the new Norman settlers under the earl of Chester. Caradog ap Gruffudd also retired
from war, at least for a couple of years. We do not know why, as
his pressure on Deheubarth had been continuous, and his designs
upon its kingship considerable. Perhaps his Norman neighbours
were proving troublesome, perhaps he needed time to allow his warriors to heal and rest, perhaps the weather proved unfavourable. For
whatever reason, Rhys ap Tewdwr found himself left alone by his

Welsh neighbours for the first two years of his reign. It was not a total respite: within a year of his becoming king the church of St Davids was plundered. Our sources do not tell us the identity of the raiders, but at this period they are likely to have been one or other of the several Viking groups which were operating within the Irish Sea area.[98] Rhys was almost certainly not on the spot to meet the raiders. Churches were a favourite target for opportunistic attacks, as they provided convenient conglomerations of valuables (church plate and offerings), foodstuffs and men (potential slaves), and often lacked strong defences. That a church within Deheubarth was attacked tells us little about Rhys' power. St Davids was coastal and readily accessible to sea-born attackers. It had been targeted before, in 810; in 907 when the effective Cadell ap Rhodri Mawr ruled Deheubarth; in 981 in the reign of Owain ap Hywel Dda; and in 999 during the reign of Maredudd ab Owain. It was hard for a king of Deheubarth to arrive at the church in time to defend it: by the time news of a raid reached him, the Vikings were probably long gone. In the first two years of his reign, Rhys probably spent his time consolidating his control over the kingdom and trying to improve and strengthen his links with the local nobility.

1081 was to prove the crisis year for his kingship. Caradog ap Gruffudd remained king of Morgannwg and had by no means forgotten his ambitions regarding Deheubarth. In 1081, he launched a renewed onslaught. As before, he was aided by his ally from Gwynedd, Trahaearn ap Caradog, and the latter was now accompanied by a man who may have been his heir or his *penteulu*, Meilyr ap Rhiwallon. Meilyr was the son of Rhiwallon ap Cynfyn, co-ruler 1064–1069 of Gwynedd and Powys with his brother Bleddyn, and a kinsman of Trahaearn.[99] The Line of Bleddyn took an interest in at least the northern parts of Deheubarth, and especially in the debatable territory of Ceredigion, which passed frequently between Deheubarth, Powys and Gwynedd. One can easily imagine that Caradog, Meilyr and Trahaearn were bent upon dividing Deheubarth between them.

It was a redoubtable combination of aggressors, with substantial forces at their disposal. Trahaearn and Caradog were both seasoned commanders who probably commanded considerable loyalty from their nobility and could draw support from wide areas.[100] Rhys was still a relatively new quantity in Deheubarth, and he may not have been certain of all of his *uchelwyr*. But he found himself with an ally of his own. This was Gruffudd ap Cynan, the claimant from the Line of Merfyn to Gwynedd.[101] Raised in Ireland, Gruffudd had little or no support base in Wales, and had already made one unsuccessful attempt to establish himself in Gwynedd in 1075. What he did possess was Hiberno-Scandinavian kinsmen who were able to supply him with mercenary forces. In 1081, having been absent from Wales for six years, Gruffudd came to St Davids, accompanied by a Viking fleet.

According to the twelfth-century biography of Gruffudd, Rhys came to meet him at the church in a state of great distress. Greeting Gruffudd as 'king of the kings of Wales',[102] Rhys related how he had been routed by Caradog and his allies. Gruffudd asked him what he would give in return for aid against these enemies, and received a promise of homage and half of Rhys' kingdom. This version was doubtless gratifying to the descendants of Gruffudd ap Cynan, under whose auspices the biography was probably composed, but is highly unlikely to be realistic. In the first place, although Rhys faced invasion, his position within Wales was stronger than Gruffudd's. He was in possession of his kingdom and its resources. Our other sources, which represent a more contemporary layer of recording than the biography of Gruffudd, make no mention of any rout of Rhys by Caradog and his forces. Gruffudd, on the other hand, had few or no supporters within Wales, and, arriving as he did with a Viking fleet, was likely to be an object of distrust. Moreover, the language of the biography is anachronistic: homage is a concept which arrived in Wales with the expansion of Norman power. By 1081, their influence was not so widely felt. It is almost certain that Rhys would not have made an offer of that type in those terms. The description of the biography pre-supposes that Gruffudd's identity was widely known and accepted, yet the Chronicles refer to him as 'grandson of Iago', suggesting that he had, at this period, to be identified by recourse to a man who had been dead for 30 years. Nor does their account of Trahaearn imply any discontent with him, any sense of him as a usurper or false king, or of Gruffudd as a rightful heir. The author of the biography wrote long after the events he described and had no first hand knowledge of them or of the men involved in them. He wrote against a very different political landscape, in a time when Norman settlement in Wales – and particularly in south Wales – was advanced. The rulers of Deheubarth no longer styled themselves as kings, and no longer disposed of the valuable low-lands in the southern part of the former kingdom: in the first part of the twelfth century, their power had been eclipsed completely. They regained some of their power and status during the later twelfth century under the gifted Rhys ap Gruffudd, the Lord Rhys, nephew to Nest. But the writer of the biography was not concerned with the fluctuations of Deheubarth but with the glorification of the princes of Gwynedd. By presenting Rhys ap Tewdwr – grandfather of the Lord Rhys – offering submission to Gruffudd ap Cynan, the biographer sought to enhance and support the claims to the overlordship of Wales of the descendants of Gruffudd. His picture should therefore be interpreted in this light, and not as a direct reflection of eleventh-century realities.

We should, rather, envisage Gruffudd as the junior partner in the alliance. He could bring armed men to the conflict, but he was probably less experienced in war than Rhys, and he had few or no social or political ties to the native nobility. The battle that ensued between the forces of Rhys and those of Caradog ap Gruffudd, moreover, was almost certainly located in northern Deheubarth or its borders.[103]

It is known to history as the battle of Mynydd Carn, and its effects on the Welsh political landscape were to prove critical. By the standards of the period, it was a massive encounter, involving the military forces of all the four major kingdoms of Wales, supplemented by Gruffudd ap Cynan's Vikings and perhaps Norman archers under Caradog. It should not be imagined as a mere skirmish: of the five named participants, three lost their lives, and it is highly likely that many in their personal warbands and perhaps also of their armies died alongside them. By the end, Trahaearn, Caradog and Meilyr all lay dead. It was in some ways an extraordinary victory for Gruffudd and Rhys: they were less experienced less established, and probably out-numbered. On the other hand, Rhys, at least, was probably on familiar territory, and his men may have been fresher than those of his enemies, who would have had to travel considerable distances and who may have faced problems of supply and of support from the lands through which they passed.

His victory at Mynydd Carn left Rhys without any immediate rival in the south, and took the pressure off his northern borders. For Gruffudd, the consequences proved less positive. He journeyed north to lay claim to Gwynedd, only to fall into the hands of Robert of Rhuddlan, who imprisoned him for somewhere between twelve and sixteen years. This was perhaps the first sign that Mynydd Carn had a significance that was wider than Wales. The year 1081 had already proved to be an important one for Rhys, but another event was to make it extraordinary.

Here is the account of the Welsh language chronicle *Brut y Tywysogyon*:

Ac yna y deuth Gwilim Bastard, brenhin y Saesson a'r Freinc a'r Brytanyeit, wrth wediaw drwy bererindawt y Vynyw.

And then William the Bastard, king of the Saxons and the French and the Britons came on a pilgrimage to Menevia to offer prayers.[104]

At first sight, it is hard to see why this apparent record of a religious visit to St Davids by William the Conqueror might have more than peripheral consequences for Rhys. But its significance is immense. In the first instance, no English king that we know of had ever come to St Davids, be it for reasons of prayer or of politics. We know of no tradition of pilgrimage to that church current outside Wales at this period, nor is it easy to imagine why the Norman William would specifically wish to pay his respects to a saint who must have been very obscure to him. When kings of England came to Wales, they did so with warlike intent, and when they wished to parley, they expected Welsh kings to come to them on or near the borders of Wales with England.[105] What we have here is the explanation of a chronicler, probably a cleric, of an event which was both unprecedented and perhaps superficially incomprehensible save in these religious terms.

Why did William come to south Wales? It was almost certainly on account of the upheaval caused by Mynydd Carn.[106] We know that Caradog ap Gruffudd had had involvement with the Normans in Herefordshire and perhaps Gloucestershire, sometimes hostile, sometimes more co-operative. To the north, Trahaearn had faced incursions into his lands by Robert of Rhuddlan and the earl of Chester. In the later 1060s and early 1070s, Welsh rulers – notably Bleddyn ap Cynfyn – had assisted Anglo-Saxon rebels against William.[107] There was no guarantee that this would not recur. We do not know if William, his earls or their representatives had had agreements of any kind with either Caradog or Trahaearn: it may be that during the later 1070s the struggle between these two and Rhys ab Owain served as a distraction which reduced any potential threat from Wales to Norman lands near the border. But Mynydd Carn had removed both Trahaearn and Caradog, and left Rhys ap Tewdwr as the most powerful king within Wales. And to the Norman king and his men, Rhys must have been an unknown quantity.

William seems to have pursued a fairly non-interventionist policy towards Wales. In the early years of his reign he had taken steps to secure the border, and he sanctioned a degree of incursion by his men into Welsh territories, but he does not seem to have intended any immediate conquest of Wales. He had other concerns. In the wake of Mynydd Carn, he seems to have taken no action to stem the ambitions of the earl of Chester and Robert of Rhuddlan in Gwynedd and Powys, nor did he object to the seizure and imprisonment of Gruffudd ap Cynan. But the earl of Chester, Hugh d'Avranches, was a trusted advisor and vassal. William lacked a similar reliable earl on the southern Welsh border. He had installed the loyal and dependable William fitz Osbern as earl of Hereford in 1067, but William had died around 1071 and his son and successor Roger de Breteuil had proved disloyal, rebelling against William in 1075. William had deprived him of the earldom, exiled him, and since then Herefordshire had been administered on the king's behalf by royal officials. But he possessed no one strong vassal in the area to put up a firm defence against any threat that Rhys ap Tewdwr might present. He needed to find out more about Rhys and to enter into a relationship of some kind with him which would secure his good behaviour regarding Norman border lands.

This was almost certainly the purpose of his trip to St Davids: not prayer, but politics. The bishops of St Davids lay outside the formal administrative structure of the church within England at this time, but they did have contact with English bishops and archbishops. A church – in particular the most prominent church in Wales – made a reassuring location for a meeting between the king of England and the new ruler of Deheubarth. The bishop might have made an appropriate mediator, moreover: it is unlikely that Rhys spoke Norman French, and William spoke no Welsh, but the two would have been able to communicate via clergy (who would use Latin), or perhaps through English-speaking interpreters. William almost certainly came to St Davids by sea: the alternative land journey through Wales would have taken longer and presented more dangers. William cannot have been sure of a warm welcome, nor that Rhys had control over the Welsh lords of south-east and central Wales. It is likely that under the auspices of St Davids, a deal was brokered between William and Rhys. What were the terms? We cannot know for sure, but it will probably have included guarantees to Rhys that he and his lands would remain unmolested by William's vassals. In return, he may well have undertaken not to harass the Norman settlers in the border, in the south-east or in north Wales. He also seems to have made some kind of submission to William as his overlord, perhaps even entering some kind of feudal relationship. *Domesday Book*, compiled five years later for William, records that forty pounds was paid to the king by 'Riset de Wales' – who can only have been Rhys ap Tewdwr.[108] Did Rhys actually make such a payment on a regular basis – or at all? We do not know. The figure is matched by a forty-pound sum owed for north Wales by Robert of Rhuddlan, and may represent tidiness on behalf of the compilers more than reality.

In 1079, when he became king, Rhys' position may well have seemed tenuous; however, by the end of 1081, he must have felt far more secure. His rivals were dead, and he had been granted the sanction of the powerful king of England. It is probably at around this time that he married – or perhaps remarried.[109] The marriage of a king held more significance than that of a member of the warband or a nobleman. We should not rule out the possibility that Rhys had already married or had had liaisons with one or more women. But it is probably after 1081 that he made the one marriage we know of. Marriage was one of the routes by which royal and noble kindreds forged alliances and attempted to consolidate relationships. Although Trahaearn and Caradog were dead, they had left kinsmen, and it was more than likely that one or more of these would come to the fore and might attack or harass Rhys. This potential problem might be expected to be exacerbated by the fact that Norman settlements were increasing both in Gwent and in the north. Displaced nobility and scions of royal lines could very well turn their eyes westwards. The royal houses of what had been Morgannwg were in eclipse: indeed, they were never to recover after the death of Caradog, and later members of both his family and of the other, older house which his family had overshadowed were reduced to the status of minor lords, under Norman dominion. Gwynedd and Powys were another matter. Gruffudd ap Cynan was in prison, but Rhiwallon and Bleddyn, sons of Cynfyn, and their cousin Trahaearn had all left sons, some of whom were approaching manhood. Rhys had good reason to be concerned about this family, and he now took steps to reduce the likelihood of attack from them. He married Gwladus, daughter of Rhiwallon ap Cynfyn and sister of the Meilyr who had died at Mynydd Carn. She was almost certainly the mother of Nest, and of Rhys's sons Gruffudd and Hywel. Perhaps at around the same time, Rhys' shadowy brother Rhydderch married Gwladus' first cousin, Hunydd, daughter of Bleddyn ap Cynfyn. Rhydderch must

have been rather younger than Rhys, whom he seems to have out-
lived by at least twenty years, as his only recorded action was in 1115,
in which year he was involved in the defence of Carmarthen castle
against his nephew, Gruffudd ap Rhys.[110]

NEST'S CHILDHOOD IN WALES

This, then, was the background against which Nest was born. We
do not know the year of her birth: Welsh Chronicles and records
at that period did not note such things. We know that she was an
adult woman with children by 1115, and we know the death dates of
at least some of her children.[111] Her brother Gruffudd died in 1137,
but we do not possess Nest's own date of death. She must have been
conceived, if not born, in 1093, in which year her father was killed.
Beyond this, we cannot be sure. Her first marriage probably took
place in the first years of the twelfth century, and there are reasons to
suppose she was old enough to bear a child by this time.[112] Women
could be married relatively young at this period. Under Welsh law
a girl was eligible to be married between the ages of twelve and
fourteen.[113] Under Canon Law, no girl in Anglo-Norman England
should be sent to be married before the age of twelve, but this rule
could be discounted – and sometimes was, particularly in the case of
royal marriages. Matilda, the daughter of King Henry I of England,
was sent to be married at the age of just eight. As will be seen, there
are probably reasons why Nest was not married quite so young. It is
most likely that she was born at some time between 1081 and around
1085.

Welsh girls were reared at home, unlike their counterparts in
Ireland, who were sent out for fosterage.[114] As was described earlier, we should imagine Nest as a young child living in her father's
various houses, travelling with the court and perhaps seeing him
administer justice, feast his warriors and greet visitors. She would not
have been referred to as 'princess', nor, probably, would her mother
have been called a queen. These titles were not used in eleventh-

century Wales. Their status was defined and referred to in relation to
Rhys – the king's daughter, the king's wife. The use of a royal title for
women is not reflected within Welsh society before the late twelfth
and early thirteenth centuries. The Welsh Laws speak of the queen,
but there is no evidence for any real woman in Wales ever using or
being referred to in this way outside the laws. In the early thirteenth
century, the wife of the prince of Gwynedd is found using the title
'Lady of Wales', but she is a special case.[115] Privileged Nest certainly
was: she had rights and a social value far greater than most other
females in Wales. But to call her a princess is a modern anachronism.

Her mother will have had her own household officers and maids
and Nest must have spent most of her time amongst them.[116] The
king's wife seems to have possessed her own chamber – sometimes
a separate building – at the royal *llysoedd* and it is within this context
that Nest received her early education.

What did this include? We have little or no information about the
education of children within Wales in the medieval period, and such
as we do have relates largely to boys. The *Life of Samson*, a saint mainly
associated with Brittany, but supposedly born and educated in Wales,
describes the saint as a boy studying in a school run by another saint,
Illtud. The young boy is instructed in scripture, rhetoric, grammar and
arithmetic, as well as in the writings of the Church Fathers.[117] Saint
Teilo was taught to read scripture by St Dyfrig, according to the *Life
of Teilo*, which dates to the early twelfth century. But these accounts
are written in an ecclesiastical context and in a tradition of writing
about saints. The boys are proto-saints, already placed in a religious
environment. Learning of a specific Christian kind was expected of
them. We have one Life of a female Welsh saint, Gwenfrewi, which
gives us some details of her education. Her father elected to have
her concentrate on studying for a religious life. It is not stated, however, that she was taught to read: her knowledge may, as has been
pointed out by Ceridwen Lloyd-Morgan, have been oral.[118] The *Life
of Gwenfrewi* is, moreover, one of the latest of our surviving Welsh
Saints' Lives, and is considerably removed in time from the realities of the lifetimes of either Gwenfrewi (who, if she existed, would

date to perhaps the seventh century), or Nest. The writers of Saints' Lives, moreover, wrote to a considerable degree within a defined genre, which laid out an expected pattern for the development of the saint – his education and teachers and influences, his travels, his relations with secular lords, his church or churches, his miracles and so forth. The Lives were often written long after the events they purport to describe and with a didactic purpose. They were meant to teach lessons about proper Christian conduct and about the respect due to the saint and the churches associated with him, rather than act as straight biographies. Saints were always extraordinary people whose backgrounds and experiences were different from the norm. Descriptions of their education cannot be taken as a reliable guide to the experience of non-religious figures. The biography of Gruffudd ap Cynan, perhaps significantly, relates a great deal about his ancestry, Welsh, Irish and Scandinavian, and about the military and political prowess of several of his male forebears. But all we hear of his upbringing is that he was 'a lad of good manners and sumptuous upbringing', and that his mother took care to tell him 'who and what kind of man his father was, what patrimony belonged to him, what kind of kingdom, and what kind of oppressors were inhabiting it.'[119] The concern is not with his intellectual abilities but with his noble blood, his rights and his courage. As an adult, he is gifted in war, moderate in peace, generous to all, and a sponsor of the church. The qualities desired and praised in a lord or king were far different to those expected from saints. Kings might be generous to churches and monasteries, but they were not expected to partake of monastic ideas of learning.

What can we learn of childhood in Wales from the prose tales and the law codes? Again, we hear a great deal more about boys than about girls. In *Pwyll*, we are told that Pwyll's son Pryderi was unusually big for his age and grew faster than average. He was stronger than other boys. But as to his education, the tale says only that 'he was brought up carefully, as was proper, until he was the most perfect lad and the handsomest and the most accomplished at every feat in the kingdom.'[120] Similarly, the young Lleu Llawr Gyffes, in *Math,* is bigger and faster-growing that other boys his age, but the only detail given about his education is that he was taught to ride any horse.[121] As to Culhwch, the protagonist of *Culhwch ac Olwen*, the tale relates only that he was well-born. The only girls we meet are young women of marriageable age. We are told nothing about their education, only about their appearance, social skills, nobility of birth and virginity. The prose tales paint the same picture as the biography of Gruffudd ap Cynan, emphasising physical skills and blood over learning.

The Law Codes are, as has been said, depicting an ideal situation – society as it ought to be, described in a formalised and specifically legal fashion. Children in the laws thus appear predominantly in terms of their social position, their worth, their inheritance rights and who was responsible for them. Early Wales was a *weregild* culture: each individual was ascribed a specific value which could be expressed in economic terms. The value of a given person had two facets: physical, *galanas* – the amount which their body or its constituent elements was deemed to have; and face or honour, *sarhaed* – the amount that person was worth in terms of their social standing. In both cases, the amounts were calculated based on the individual's *braint*, status in the social hierarchy. Children were valued in terms of the social standing of their fathers, and girls were considered as of less value than their brothers.[122] As the daughter of a king, Nest would have been one of the most valuable girl children in Wales.

The Law Codes tell us a great deal concerning property rights, and these can give us some clues as to the sorts of activities and skills expected of women.[123] Much of the property over which a woman had rights relates to domestic and private activities – items such as certain cooking vessels, personal clothing and ornaments and food from her larder.[124] We know, too, that one of the personnel of the royal court was the baker, who was expected to be female. Nest would have grown up in a domestic atmosphere, concerned with cooking and the production and care of garments. Girls brought up in the families of bond, tenant or free farmers probably had to do their share of farm work, be it watching over animals, collecting eggs, milking, assisting with harvesting crops, growing and preparing vegetables, and gathering fruit, nuts and perhaps firewood. It is likely Nest was exempt from most of these tasks. She would, however, have been taught to sew and embroider and perhaps to spin and weave, to prepare at least some types of food and – perhaps most importantly – how to conduct herself in social situations.

Was she literate? It is very hard to know. As has been described, the only boys whose education explicitly included literacy in our sources are those associated with the church. We hear of saints, but at least some boys intended for the clergy may have received a church education.[125] In England and on the continent, some daughters of kings and noblemen were sent to convents to train as nuns, and these girls will have received at least some education, probably including some level of literacy. Indeed, some daughters of royal or high noble families were sent to convents for education before marriage, as was the case with Henry I's future queen, Edith-Matilda. Wales, however, had no tradition of convents or nunneries before the later twelfth and thirteenth centuries.[126] Such religious training as Nest received will have been from the priest attached to the *llys*, and there is no reason to suppose that this included reading or writing, for Nest, or, indeed, for her brothers. We have only the tenuous evidence of the *Life of Gwenfrewi* to hint at a possibility that some girls of high birth may have been taught at least some basic reading or writing skills. Such evidence we have as to female ownership of books or of nuns within Wales all relates to the end of the twelfth century and later.[127] But we should probably envisage Nest's education in her father's court as primarily social and domestic.

THE POLITICS OF NEST'S CHILDHOOD YEARS

In the wake of the battle of Mynydd Carn, Rhys ap Tewdwr found himself in a far stronger position than he had been in at the start of his rule. The next few years saw a degree of peace within his lands not seen since the later years of Gruffudd ap Llywelyn. Between

1081 and 1087, as far as we know from our extant records, no threats arose to challenge his power and control. The native lines of the other Welsh kingdoms were in eclipse and those Normans who were bound on settlement within Wales were occupied in the south-east and in Gwynedd. As Babcock has suggested, Rhys probably spent these years in managing his lands, strengthening his ties with the nobility, travelling from *llys* to *llys* and administering justice.[128] It was probably in these years, as we have seen, that Nest and her brothers were born, and in which she would have seen the Welsh governmental system in operation. This seven-year period was, arguably, the last flowering of the old Welsh royal way of life, before Norman influences and practices changed it forever. We cannot know if Rhys anticipated a long reign; however, he probably did not expect to enjoy peace for the rest of his life. His own experience under his cousins, Maredudd, Rhys and Hywel, sons of Owain, and the past history of kingship in Wales argued against it. Military leadership was a key element in Welsh kingship, and one that was expected to be exercised frequently.

In 1087, William the Conqueror died, and was succeeded in England by his second son, William Rufus. The news will certainly have reached Rhys, but it is hard to guess what he initially thought of it. William the Conqueror had not interfered with him since their agreement in 1081, at least as far as we know. Rhys may have thought that this state of affairs would continue under William Rufus. And then, the accession of William Rufus had not been unanimously welcomed by the Anglo-Norman nobility, some of whom would have preferred his elder brother, Robert Curthose.[129] Within months of William Rufus's accession, a significant section of his aristocracy went into rebellion against him. The rebels included Roger of Montgomery, the Earl of Shrewsbury, who had substantial interests in east and central Wales; Ralph Mortimer, Lord of Wigmore, on the Welsh border; Osbern fitzRichard, Lord of Richard's Castle in west Herefordshire and husband of Gruffudd ap Llywelyn's daughter Nest; and Roger de Lacey, the new Lord of Weobley. Hugh d'Avranches, the Earl of Chester, remained loyal to William Rufus and became

involved in fighting on the royal side. With many of the border magnates occupied with this rebellion, their attention was diverted from
Wales.[130] Rhys may even have hoped that the rebellion would last, or
that the English crown would be substantially weakened, allowing
him the opportunity to expand eastwards, back into lands which had
been overshadowed by Norman lords. As will be seen, indeed, he
may even have begun to make moves in that direction.

In 1088, the peace enjoyed by Deheubarth came to an end, and
in a dramatic way. The kingdom was invaded by Madog, Rhirid and
Cadwgan, three of the six known sons of the former king of Powys
and Gwynedd, Bleddyn ap Cynfyn. They had grown up in a Powys
under considerable Norman pressure and must have spent their
childhood watching their father's lands being colonised. The events
of the first years of the twelfth century suggest that they had probably
already developed a relationship of some kind, however grudging,
with their powerful eastern neighbour, the Earl of Shrewbury, Roger
of Montgomery and his sons. But in 1088, Roger's attention was
still elsewhere, with his involvement in the rebellion against William
Rufus and its consequences. The sons of Bleddyn were presented
with a chance to take action without the danger of attracting rapid
reaction from Earl Roger. They also saw an opportunity to expand
their interests or acquire new lands to replace those lost to the
Normans. They cannot have been totally landless, as they clearly had
access to sufficient resources to muster an army and maintain a warband, and the events of the twelfth century were to prove that they
possessed considerable support in their family heartlands. They were
also men of ambition, who had not lost sight of the extent of their
father's hegemony and the success of his rule.

Rhys ap Tewdwr seems to have been taken by surprise. By his
marriage, he had hoped to secure good relations with the Line of
Bleddyn. Certainly, he seems to have been unprepared for the invasion. Perhaps he did not have time to muster an army and had only
his *teulu* with him. The sons of Bleddyn swept into Deheubarth and
drove Rhys out entirely. He fled to Ireland – as he may have done in
his youth – and took refuge. We do not know exactly where he went

in Ireland, but it must have been one of the Hiberno-Scandinavian towns,[131] as he promptly raised a mercenary fleet to aid him, and sailed back for Wales. He met the sons of Bleddyn in battle at a place referred to by our surviving records as *Penletheru* or *Llechycrau*.[132] The Welsh Chronicles do not tell us if any of the nobility of Deheubarth came to meet him, but he won the battle. Madog and Rhirid were killed, and Cadwgan retreated, leaving Rhys once again in power. We do not know what became of Rhys' immediate family during his short exile. It is most likely that they remained on one of the royal estates or in the care of a trusted *uchelwyr*. Nest may well have been too young to understand what was happening, but this was her first taste of the conflict and rivalry which was all too common in early medieval Wales.

The victory left Rhys once again king, but it also created something of a problem for him. The presence of an invading army and the conflict it brought with it will have had consequences for the local economy. Crops will have been damaged, destroyed or seized, livestock driven off or impounded, valuables plundered. If the fighting occurred during the planting or harvesting seasons, the cereal yield for the year will have been reduced, as men were summoned to fight, rather than farm. Rhys' personal wealth, or some parts of it, may well have been carried off by the invaders. Yet Rhys' men – and his hired fleet – required reward, and this would be expected to be swiftly forthcoming. The Welsh language Chronicles, the *Brutiau*, tell us that he gave treasure to his fleet of Hiberno-Scandinavians, but the Latin Chronicles, the *Annales Cambriae*, which represent an earlier layer of recording, omit this detail.[133] Did he fail to pay, or to pay quickly enough? It is possible. The following year, 1089, an unidentified force raided and plundered St Davids. Indeed, the *Annales Cambriae* place this raid in the same year as the invasion.[134] It is entirely possible that the raiders were none other than Rhys' former allies, seeking payment. It may be, also, that Rhys had rewarded them, but they had been unsatisfied with what they had received.

We do not know what Nest knew of these events. Perhaps she saw the Hiberno-Scandinavian mercenaries after the victory, being feasted with the *teulu* in one of her father's halls. Her brothers Gruffudd and Hywel, if they were then old enough, may have had a chance to speak with some of them, although Gruffudd could not have known then that he was to spend many years with such men in their Irish home towns. At the very least, Nest and her brothers must have been aware of a reduction of anxiety amongst the adults around them, and pleased to see their father return safely.

The invasion weakened Rhys and in its wake it appears that his support base began to wane. He was ageing and he perhaps appeared less effective. And then, a new adult claimant to his throne was waiting in the wings, in the person of Gruffudd ap Maredudd ap Owain, the son of Rhys's cousin Maredudd who had been killed in 1072. Gruffudd had been living in exile, on lands in England which he had inherited through his father. But it appears that he had not lost contact with the noblemen of Deheubarth.

At this period, we rarely possess information about any of the *uchelwyr*, save, perhaps, the occasional name in a pedigree. However, a chronicle entry for the year 1116 provides us with a possible insight in one at least of the noblemen of Deheubarth under Rhys.[135] This entry belongs to a section of the Welsh language annals which is particularly associated with the activities of the royal line of Powys.[136] The reference which interests here occurs in a section concerned with listing the brothers of Owain ap Cadwgan ab Bleddyn and their mothers. One of the women named is Ellylw, daughter of Cedifor ap Gollwyn, 'supreme lord over all the land of Dyfed'.[137]

Who was this Cedifor? We know from the Chronicles that he died in 1091.[138] He was not a member of the royal house of Deheubarth, but he was clearly a man of power and influence: an *uchelwyr*. Some caution should be exercised over the description of Cedifor from the entry for 1116. The section in question is at least partially retrospective and its main interest in demonstrating the legitimacy and honour of the Line of Powys. It is not beyond the bounds of possibility that the reference to Cedifor may have been embroidered in order to enhance the status of his grandson, the son of Cadwgan ab Bleddyn. Nevertheless, his death had a significant effect on Rhys, so although he may not have been 'supreme lord' he must have been influential. Babcock has argued that he must have been one of the senior noblemen in Dyfed, powerful enough to wield wide control over the southern part of Deheubarth, and an important supporter of Rhys, and that his sons were for some reason dissatisfied with Rhys or with the agreement their father had had with him.[139] They allied themselves with Gruffudd ap Maredudd and summoned him to return to Deheubarth and mount an challenge for the kingship. If the influence of Cedifor was genuinely as widespread in Dyfed as the Welsh language chronicles suggest, then Rhys may have found himself facing what amounted to an insurrection in half of his kingdom. It seems more likely, however, that Gruffudd obtained the support only of the sons of Cedifor and their immediate circle, as his attempt at acquiring power was to be short-lived. Rhys marched to meet him with his own army and the two sides met in battle at Llandudoch, close to modern Cardigan. This coastal location suggests that Gruffudd may have arrived by sea, which raises the possibility that he may have garnered at least a little support from the Anglo-Normans of Herefordshire, where his lands lay. There is no trace of this in any other record, and if such aid did occur, it must have been small-scale. Alternatively, Gruffudd may have been able to hire a ship from the port at Bristol. He was not to meet with success, whoever his additional supporters may have been. Rhys defeated him in battle, and the fighting cost Gruffudd his life.

That Gruffudd may have had at least a little support from the Norman lords of the border cannot be proved, but it should be considered as at least a possibility. The rebellion against William Rufus was over, but the new king needed ways to reward his loyal allies and to encourage former rebels against any further rebellion. He needed, also, to find an outlet for their ambitions and their desire to gain new lands and resources. The process of Norman incursion and settlement in Wales had begun as early as 1067 and, in the former Morgannwg and in Gwynedd, had continued through the reign of William the Conqueror. Only the south-west was protected, through the old agreement between the Conqueror and Rhys ap Tewdwr. It may be, also, that Rhys had not entirely upheld whatever his side of the bargain was. We have no indication that he made any attempt to indicate submission to the new king of England, and William Rufus may perhaps have assumed that he was simply another rebel. Then, while the Normans regarded submission as binding and permanent, the Welsh did not. Vassalage was not a part of their political system; rather, a lord or king might agree to recognise another as overlord, but this was considered to hold only for as long as both parties felt the agreement to be to their advantage. As we have seen with the sons of Cedifor, if a nobleman – or a king – became dissatisfied with their overlord, they would withdraw their support. Rhys almost certainly took his relationship with William the Conqueror as personal, and did not expect it to carry over to William's son.

Perhaps, if William Rufus's accession had gone unchallenged, or if there had been a major war elsewhere – within Normandy, or on the border with Scotland – Rhys might have been safe in his assumptions. But circumstances within the Anglo-Norman state were against him.

On the south central border of Wales lay the ancient kingdom of Brycheiniog. This had originally possessed its own royal line, but it was one of the territories overrun by the Line of Merfyn, and it had long ceased to have an independent existence, becoming instead a debatable land between Powys, Deheubarth and Morgannwg. By 1093, Norman settlers were establishing themselves at least in its eastern districts. Their lord was Bernard of Neufmarché, one of the men who had rebelled against William Rufus at the start of his reign. His movement into Brycheiniog probably began in 1088, after the quashing of the rebellion.[140] Bernard may only have arrived in England at the very end of the reign of William the Conqueror. Certainly, we have no evidence for his presence before 1086, but by 1088 he had lands in Herefordshire plus an estate at Glasbury, which technically lay within the borders of Wales.[141] He may have owed some of his Herefordshire lands to his marriage: his new wife was Nest, daughter of Osbern fitzRichard of Richard's Castle (who had married Nest, the daughter of Gruffudd ap Llywelyn).[142] Perhaps Bernard justified his incursion into Wales on the grounds that his wife was partly Welsh. It is more likely, however, that he was simply ambitious and Brycheiniog was easily accessible from his new lands. The Wye valley provided fertile and desirable land. It is likely, as Nelson has proposed, that he did so with the tacit sanction of William Rufus. The annexation of Welsh lands provided a useful distraction for the energies of a man who had shown himself ready to rebel, but who was neither personally sufficiently powerful nor very strongly tied to William's rival Robert Curthose to require dispossession.[143] We know he had acquired Glasbury by 1088, for in that year he granted it to the church of St Peter's, Gloucester. By 1093, his conquest was well-advanced and it must have begun to trouble Rhys ap Tewdwr, who was, after all, the most powerful leader within native Wales and the sole reigning king of any of its kingdoms. We do not know how far east Rhys' personal influence extended. It is highly unlikely he had any direct control in Brycheiniog, but some of its native noblemen may well have considered him a preferable option as overlord to the Normans of the border.

Perhaps the leading men of Brycheiniog summoned him, perhaps he went into Brycheiniog on his own initiative, intending to give a check to Norman ambitions. We do not know. But we do know that in the week around Easter in 1093 (17–23 April), Rhys ap Tewdwr came to Aberhonddu, modern Brecon, with an army, close to where the Normans were building a castle.[144] And then, as *Brut y Tywysogyon* relates:

> Rhys ap Tewdwr, king of the South, was slain by the Frenchmen who inhabited Brycheiniog – with whom fell the kingdom of the Britons … And within two months of that, the French overran Dyfed and Ceredigion … and made castles in them and fortified them. And then the French seized all the lands of the Britons.[145]

2

NEST'S GIRLHOOD

The death in battle of her father changed Nest's world forever. The importance of Rhys' death was clear even to the Normans who desired his lands, and his fall in battle was recorded by the Anglo-Norman historian John of Worcester who, like the Welsh author of *Brut y Tywysogyon*, considered it to mark the end of truly independent Wales. The final conquest of native Wales in 1283 by Edward I is in many ways foreshadowed by the downfall of Rhys ap Tewdwr, as subsequent kings and princes had to adapt their policies and behaviour to Anglo-Norman and Angevin claims of dominance.

The immediate consequences were cataclysmic. Within a matter of months, all of Rhys' former kingdom had been overrun by Norman lords from the border counties. In the north, Gruffudd ap Cynan still languished in prison. The only royal Welshman who was of age, active and still free was the determined Cadwgan ab Bleddyn from Powys, who had invaded Deheubarth with his brothers in 1088, and he, almost certainly, had had to enter into some kind of quasi-feudal relationship with his most powerful Norman neighbour, Roger of Montgomery, Earl of Shrewsbury. Cadwgan had by no means abandoned his ambitions on the south-west, and before Rhys ap Tewdwr had been dead for a month, he was once more in Deheubarth with his army, plundering, and, probably, seeking to annex as much as he might to his own power. But the Norman lords of the border had no intention of seeing a new king arise in south-west Wales. In July of 1093, a Norman army bound upon conquest came to Deheubarth and Ceredigion, determined to seize the land for themselves.

To the child Nest, it must have seemed as if the world was ending. The remnants of her father's forces presumably made their way back within days of the battle near Brecon, bearing the news of the death of Rhys. Did she mourn her father? We have no information as to the nature of their relationship. We do know that, unlike in Ireland, girls in medieval Wales were not sent out for fosterage but remained with their parents – the phrase used by the law codes is 'at her father's platter'[1] – until they were between twelve and fourteen, at which age they would be sent to be married or to work in another's house. The image this conjures is one of intimacy: of the daughter eating with her parents in a family environment. While daughters held less social value than sons, there is nothing in our extant evidence to suggest that they were not usually treated with affection. It is to be hoped that the relationship between Nest and Rhys was a warm one. Certainly, it appears that in adulthood she was proud of her Welshness: if her experiences at her father's court in young childhood had been very unpleasant, she may well have felt differently.[2] We do not know how old she and her brothers were in the spring of 1093 – it is likely that none of them were more than eleven or twelve – but they must have been aware that their position was now very uncertain. For the first few days, considerable chaos may have reigned in Rhys' hall.

The sons of Rhys were too young to be made king, but he had had a brother, Rhydderch, and we know he must have survived the battle at Brecon (if, indeed, he participated) as he was still alive in 1116. Perhaps at first it was expected that Rhydderch would take the kingship. We do not know. Nest's mother, Gwladus, and her household must have known, however, that they were very unlikely to go undisturbed. Cadwgan ab Bleddyn was her first cousin and perhaps she hoped he would leave her and her children alone, at least at first, and, indeed, we do not know that he made any attempt to molest them. His invasion doubtless added to the fear and destruction, but it was of a familiar kind, part of the old pattern of raids and counter-raids which had always been part of Welsh political life. We should probably envisage Gwladus and her children taking refuge, perhaps with a loyal supporter, perhaps in a church community. But she and her circle must have been aware of the Norman threat.

At some point, Gruffudd, the elder of the two sons of Rhys ap Tewdwr, was taken by kinsmen to Ireland for refuge: we know this from Welsh Chronicles.[3] It is very probable that they fled sometime between April and July of 1109. Rhydderch ap Tewdwr may have escorted him, and perhaps it was Rhys ap Tewdwr's former Hiberno-Scandinavian employees from 1088 who fostered him. The younger son, Hywel, remained in Wales. It is likely he was too young to travel so far safely. Nest also remained. As a daughter, she had no right under Welsh law to inherit her father's lands herself, let alone any claim on the kingship of Deheubarth. She was also legally unable to transmit any such claim to a husband or son. She would, however, make a useful marriage token once she was old enough for whoever had fosterage of her. Perhaps Gwladus expected her cousin Cadwgan to find a husband for Nest: she may even have intended her daughter for one of his younger brothers or even sons.[4] Alternatively, by marrying Nest to one of the more powerful *uchelwyr* of Deheubarth – or to one of their sons – she might be able to provide her elder son with useful supporters and allies on their return from Ireland. Her own position was hardly secure: her marriage had transferred responsibility for her wellbeing from her birth family to her husband and his kin. Her sons were too young, and she must at first have been dependent upon Rhydderch. It is likely she hoped to remarry: this seems to have been the main option for royal widows in Wales at this period, regardless of whether or not they already had children. Gwladus' grandmother, Angharad, had done precisely that in the second quarter of the eleventh century. Her first marriage had been to Llywelyn ap Seisyll, but on his death she married into the nobility of Powys, and bore to her second husband Cynfyn ap Gwerystan Bleddyn and Rhiwallon (the latter being Gwladus' father). As we have seen, in Wales in the eleventh century, the cloister was not an option.

There was no tradition of wealthy widows taking holy vows and entering convents. Had her sons been adult, Gwladus could have depended upon them for support, but in the circumstances of 1093, she must have been looking out for a new husband as her only reliable means of survival.

In 1093, the Normans were a threat, but they were not the first foreigners to try and conquer or settle Welsh lands. Irish settlers had arrived in the fourth, fifth and sixth centuries, and been repulsed or absorbed. Anglo-Saxon kings and noblemen had made incursions, and been driven out or out-waited. Viking bands had built small coastal settlements, but any attempts they made at political overlordship had been thwarted. Welsh leaders like Cadwgan may well have thought that, in the long run, they would overcome the Normans also.

Who were the Norman leaders who arrived in Deheubarth and Ceredigion in 1093 and began building settlements and castles to guard them? From later evidence, Roger of Montgomery, Earl of Shrewsbury was one of them, and probably the most important. Although he already held major lands in both England and Normandy, he had six sons and he wished to see all of them comfortably and lucratively established. The eldest, Robert, would inherit his Norman lands, and the second, Hugh, his English ones, while the third, Roger, had made a good marriage. However, in the summer of 1093, yet another of his sons, Arnulf, still had no patrimony. By the invasion of Deheubarth, Roger doubtless hoped not only to increase his own wealth and standing but to provide for Arnulf. He would have been accompanied in the invasion by some of his feudal vassals from his English earldom and by other Norman lords seeking new lands and resources. Of his sons, certainly Arnulf and probably Hugh accompanied him.

Castles still stand in many of the places where this first wave of invaders sited them, but their present form generally reflects later stages of building. The first castles would have been built of wood and earth, constructed quickly to provide a strong defensive location to contain a garrison who could then control, conquer and dominate the surrounding area. Gerald of Wales described the first castle at Pembroke, which became the centre of Arnulf of Montgomery's new lordship as, '…a fortification … from wood and turf … It was not very strong and it offered little resistance.'[5] But, as Lloyd pointed out, if its initial construction was flimsy, it was placed on an unusually strong and defensible site. Gerald goes on to relate how, shortly after its construction, Pembroke was besieged by the Welsh. The castle was under the command of Gerald of Windsor, representing Arnulf:

> The siege lasted a long time, and those inside were greatly reduced and near the end of their tether. When they had hardly any provisions left, Gerald … created the impression that they were still well supplied and were expecting reinforcements at any moment: for he took four hogs, which were all they had, cut them into sections and hurled them over the palisade at the besiegers. The following day … He signed a letter with his own seal and had it placed just outside the lodging of Wilfred, bishop of St Davids … There is would be picked up almost immediately and the finder would imagine that it had been dropped accidentally by one of Gerald's messengers. The purport was that the constable would have no need of reinforcements from Arnulf for a good four months.[6]

Gerald of Wales is not the most unbiased witness to this incident, which, moreover, occurred some fifty years before his birth. Gerald the constable was his maternal grandfather and namesake: family traditions as to his heroism and intelligence doubtless grew over time. Nevertheless, this anecdote provides us with a flavour of the dangers faced by the Norman invaders in their early years. As Ifor Rowlands has observed, the initial settlement was precarious. It clustered in those areas where relief – or escape – might be, if necessary, effected by sea: Carmarthen Bay, the mouth of the River Tywi, the Cleddau estuary, and in the long peninsula of the Welsh cantref of Penfro.[7] The killing of Rhys ap Tewdwr had not prevented Welsh resistance to the invasion, and the 1090s would see a long succession of attacks, counter-attacks, battles and conflict.

What had become of Nest in the midst of all this? We do not know for certain. A possible clue, however, lies in the fate of her younger brother Hywel, as recounted by two of the Welsh language chronicles. *Brenhinedd y Saesson* and the Red Book of Hergest version of *Brut y Tywysogyon*. Under the year 1115, both relate that Hywel had been imprisoned in one of the castles belonging to Arnulf de Montgomery and there castrated.[8] They do not tell how long he had been imprisoned, but it is clear that at some point he had fallen into the hands of Arnulf, or, more probably, his men.

The imprisonment of minor male heirs was by no means uncommon at this time. Captive, they could be educated as pleased the captor, kept away from groups of individuals who might try to promote their cause and used as leverage over their kin or putative vassals. Had Hywel been killed, it might have encouraged the appearance of other claimants to Welsh Dyfed and Ystrad Tywi, but as long as he lived, he could be produced to demonstrate the existence of a legitimate heir in the face of any new challenger. Sadly, the age of the captive did not necessarily dictate their treatment, and Hywel even if a small child may well have been kept in a cell, in poor conditions. Other than his escape or release from prison, we know little more about him. In 1115, he took refuge, along with his brother Gruffudd, at the court of Gruffudd ap Cynan. After that we hear no more. Perhaps he died; more probably, he entered monastic life, which seems to have been the main option for members of royal lines who had suffered mutilation or severe injury.

He could, of course, have been captured at any time between 1093 and 1115 itself. Given the absence of any reference to him at all in our records before 1115, however, it is likely that he was seized earlier rather than later in this period. And if Hywel, who must have been a young child, was captured in the early years of the Norman invasion of the south-west, it is probable that Nest was captured with him. Welsh children were not usually given out for fostering, and a young child is unlikely to have had his own household. It seems that

Gwladus and her children came into the hands of the Norman conquerors relatively shortly after the death of Rhys ap Tewdwr.

This might have happened through chance. Equally, it may be
that the acquisition of Rhys' wife and children was a priority of
the invaders and that they were taken in the summer of 1093. It is,
however, interesting to note what became of Rhydderch ap Tewdwr,
the man who, under Welsh law, should have protected them. In
1116, when Gruffudd ap Rhys, returned from Ireland, was in rebellion, Rhydderch initially fought on the Norman side against him.
Did Rhydderch compound with the Normans in 1093 or shortly
afterwards? We do not know how old he was, but it appears he may
have had no designs on the kingship, or that he was a realist. He
must have been at least middle-aged in 1093, and may have decided
that surrendering to the invaders would protect his lands (or parts
of them) and his immediate family. It is possible that he came to
some kind of agreement with Arnulf of Montgomery or his representatives whereby he undertook neither to promote himself as
king nor his nephews – and perhaps even handed over Gwladus,
Hywel and Nest to his new overlord. In the eyes of Arnulf, Hywel
represented a potential threat: hence his imprisonment. Nest, however, was a different matter. She was unlikely to raise an army or
to find support amongst the leading men of her father's kingdom.
By 1093, the Normans had probably learnt that under Welsh law
a woman might not inherit or transmit kingship (and they would
have found nothing strange about this). But there was one key difference between the Norman and Welsh laws as regarded the daughters
of lords or kings. It was rare in the extreme for a woman in Wales
to inherit land, but to Norman eyes, an heiress was by no means
a novelty – and whoever married her could expect to control her
lands. Nest represented an extra opportunity whereby one of the
invaders might acquire and justify tenure of lands in south-west
Wales.

BEING FEMALE IN MEDIEVAL WALES

The popular image of women in Wales – and, indeed, in Ireland, pre-Saxon Britain, Scotland and any other area described as 'Celtic' – presents us with a picture of an empowered, socially equal, sexually liberated female, who might ride to war or rule a kingdom.[9] The reality, sadly, is far removed from this. Material to support the popular interpretation is gathered from a very wide selection of sources, including prose tales, accounts in late-Classical writings, ballads, poetry, archaeology, laws and later medieval romances; and these sources are drawn from a very wide area, both geographical and temporal, with the justification that all the cultures considered can be labelled as 'Celtic'. As an approach, this is methodologically troublesome for a number of reasons.

First of these is the issue of what Simon James has defined as 'Celticism' – the practice of considering as a unity a large group of peoples who either were labelled as 'Celts' by Classical authors or who may have lived in lands (or influenced these) where today languages considered Celtic are spoken, or of whom the cultural artefacts uncovered by archaeology are deemed to be Celtic in type.[10] As James has shown, the grounds for this are shaky, to say the least, and have their roots not in any ancient reality, but in the romanticism of the antiquarian movements of the eighteenth and nineteenth centuries. Moreover, the use of evidence drawn from a very wide time period – sometimes as great as from the last centuries B.C.E. to the early nineteenth century – is a risky practice, and one which tends to elide or obscure differences, external influences, recording biases and problems with transmission. To lump the Wales of the eleventh and twelfth centuries in, willy-nilly, with Roman period Gaul or seventh-century Ireland is to deny the separate histories, experiences and individuality of these places. The same is true of different times – the Britain of Boudicca is far-removed in experience, practices and contacts from the Wales of Nest – and there is no evidence to suggest that the Iceni were in any sense Nest's ancestors, or that Boudicca's cultural practices were those of Nest's ancestors.

When from the ninth century onwards the Welsh began to record in writing their own history, they show no awareness of Boudicca, her people, or her career. The circumstances in which the two women lived have superficial similarities: both faced the invasion by a foreign people of their lands. However, the differences between them are far greater. The social structures, ideas, contacts and influences the two women knew – to say nothing of the habits, practices, attitudes and expectations of their opponents – are very varied. The 'Celtic' model places these two women, who lived a thousand years apart in time, side by side in a highly inappropriate manner. In the case of Wales (and, indeed, Ireland) this issue is sometimes further complicated by the use of source materials to find or demonstrate pre-Christian practices and beliefs, and the question of women often arises very closely tied to this search. A common misconception is that pre-Christian women in Wales possessed considerable greater rights and freedoms than those from the Christian era, with the frequent implication that the apparent loss of status is a consequence of Christian practices or beliefs. Such arguments usually draw on images of women derived from prose tales, such as the Irish Queen Mebh, or the Welsh Rhiannon, who are sometimes then presented as euhemerised goddesses. In response to this it should be pointed out that the prose tales are not accounts of daily life or of normal practice, but the opposite: they deal with heroes. The life, experiences and associates of heroes are seldom, in such material, represented as anything other than extraordinary. One might, for instance, consider the list of the men of Arthur's court and their abilities which occupies a long section of *Culhwch ac Olwen*. Arthur is a figure who, it is clear, was considered to exist outside normal parameters, and his court was expected to contain extraordinary men. To the best knowledge of the present writer, it has not been suggested seriously that men in pre-Christian Wales genuinely possessed such skills. The deeds and status of a Mebh, an Arianrhod, or a Rhiannon likewise belong to this sphere of the heroic, and not to the real, yet they have all too often been used to promote the romantic image of the liberated Celtic woman. Regrettably, none of the material we possess relating to historical women supports this: this includes the records of Boudicca and Cartimandua. Both lived in times in which their culture was under extreme stress, a situation which frequently produces atypical behaviour. That a woman whose tribe faced being overwhelmed by a new culture turned to warfare does not automatically imply that other women of that tribe went to war in more normal circumstances. The accounts we have of these women from the late antique period, moreover, were written by outsiders who were both men and victors and who inevitably coloured their accounts by their own prejudices and beliefs about the 'barbarians' they described. They may have misinterpreted or misunderstood what they saw. They may have made assumptions based on pre-existing expectations of how 'barbarians' behaved – such expectations often present the object as following practices that are in opposition to the 'civilised' practices of the observer and his culture.[11] We should be very cautious before labelling these cultures described by the Roman authors as uniformly 'Celtic'. Finally, there is something of a logical contradiction to an idea that, while proposing a high degree of freedom and status for women in a pre-Christian context, also implies that, upon the introduction of the new religion – brought at first by outsiders who may not have spoken the local languages at all well – these same empowered women simply surrendered their power.[12] There is no hint in any source known to me of female resistance to Christianity in Wales (or Ireland) in such a form: had it existed, or had the pre-Christian cultures possessed such Amazonian women to begin with, it is highly unlikely that it would have left no trace at all in the sources.[13]

I propose to examine Nest not through the lens of some romantic common Celticism, but in the context which she herself would have known and accepted: that of Wales in the eleventh and twelfth centuries. The material used to consider the status, rights and position of women will likewise be drawn from Wales at this time.[14]

The main contemporary or near contemporary source for Welsh women that we possess is the surviving body of Welsh law. This survives in several manuscripts and recensions, in both Latin and

Welsh, and there are differences between these, probably reflecting differences of practice or interpretation in different parts of Wales. However, all of these various versions contain a section – referred to as a tractate – on women and the law, and called, indeed, in the Welsh language texts, *Cyfraith y Gwragedd*, the Law of Women.[15] It should be stressed that, as with any legal source of this period, the tractate presents us with an idealised picture rather than reality. The account is that of how things ought to have been, not necessarily as they have been: the real situation is usually less tidy than the legal model would suggest. Moreover, the range of situations addressed in the legal material is limited: it is interested only in those aspects of a woman's life which had legal implications. Thus we hear of how much a women is worth in law in terms of her honour-price and injury-price, but little or nothing as to how she might have spent her days, or what tasks were allotted to her. The texts are also layered – some provisions may be older than others, or may have applied in only one area of Wales. The material should thus be regarded as an outline, not as a full picture. It should also be noted that the tractate does not, by any means, contain all the legal provisions relating to or affecting women: these can be found throughout the body of medieval Welsh law.

Medieval Welsh society was hierarchical, with the king at the top and the unfree – slaves and bondsmen – at the bottom. A person's status in law depended on the rank to which they were born. The son of a bondsman was of less value than the son of a free man, and the latter was worth less than the son of a nobleman. Under the law, women in Wales occupied a lower status than men from the moment of baptism, which represented the point when they effectively became recognisable legal entities.[16] Throughout her life, a girl or woman's value was to be reckoned in terms of her male kin, and, in this instance (and down until marriage) her value was set as being one half of that of her brother.[17] Her value thus reflected both her social rank but also her femininity. As was described in Chapter One, she was raised in her father's home, no doubt participating in the daily domestic round, until she was twelve to fourteen, at which point she became eligible to be married (or, by implication, to leave home to become a servant in another household, probably that of her father's master or lord).[18] It is very unlikely that other options arose for her: as already mentioned, there was no tradition in Wales in the eleventh or twelfth century of women entering nunneries, and of the professions mentioned in the law codes the great majority are male. We meet maids, a female baker and a laundress.[19] In many cases, such women may well have been the wives of the male staff serving a lord, but, in the case of the woman baker, at least, the possibility of an unmarried female servant is mooted. We are told that if she is married, her *sarhaed* (honour-price) is one third that of her husband, if unmarried, it is half that of her brother.[20] It is impossible to know, from our surviving sources, how many unmarried women may have worked as servants in this way: it should be remembered that some such would have been from the unfree classes of Welsh society.

For most girls, save, perhaps, those born into slavery, marriage was the most significant event of their lives. Until marriage, a girl was still treated as a member of her birth family – and the latter included not only her parents and any siblings, but a wider network of relatives, all on her father's side. At the point of marriage, however, this changed.

Marriage in medieval Wales was not a matter of romance. Rather, it was a social and commercial transaction, with several layers of meaning. Certainly, it provided sexual and social companionship (in principle, at least) to the marital partners, and it looked to ensure the birth of children. However, these functions probably possessed a lesser importance than the wider ones relating to kin-groups and their interactions within society. Marriage was a strategy used by kin-groups to form bonds with one another: through a marriage, the kin-group obtained allies and supporters, reduced or cooled existing or potential conflicts, extended its influence and made gains financially or socially. We have noted that Nest's father Rhys ap Tewdwr married a woman from the royal line of Powys. This move was almost certainly intended to reduce friction between the two kingdoms and did so for at least the first years of Rhys' reign. Such marriages were quite common. Gruffudd ap Cynan, the claimant to Gwynedd,

married Angharad ferch Owain, a daughter of one of the most powerful noble families of that kingdom; Nest's brother Gruffudd was to
marry a daughter of the ruler of Gruffudd ap Cynan. Cadwgan ab
Bleddyn of Powys married another of Gruffudd's daughters, but also
the daughter of a leading nobleman of Dyfed. In the thirteenth century, Llywelyn the Great was to use the marriages of his daughters to
create for himself a network of alliances along the Welsh border: his
daughter Elen married the son of the earl of Chester; his daughter
Gwladus was given first to Reginald de Braose, the lord of lands in
Brecon, Abergavenny, Radnor and Builth and, on the latter's death,
to another powerful lord of the Welsh march, Ralph Mortimer. He
married his third daughter, Marared, to another of the Braose clan,
John. Nest's nephew, Rhys ap Gruffudd (the Lord Rhys) built himself a strong network of alliances with the nobility of south Wales by
a similar strategy of the marriages of his female kin.[21]

Marriage involved a complicated exchange of wealth between
the kin of the bride and that of her husband-to-be. The main commodity in the exchange was the bride herself, and her value in this
transaction was tightly bound with her degree of sexual experience.
She became of little or no value if she was not a virgin. If, in the
wake of the wedding night, the new husband claimed his bride was
found not to be a virgin, the evidence of her kin-group could be of
considerable importance. The kin-group was defined here as being
the bride's parents and siblings, and they could be called upon by the
bride to substantiate that she had, in fact, been a virgin. If she failed
to call upon them to support her, or if they refused her their support,
this was tantamount to a public admission of non-virginity – she
was to be considered a *twyllforwyn*, false virgin. Such a woman would
receive very different treatment to a bride who had been found to be
a virgin. A virgin wife was entitled to a settlement from her new husband, a sort of dowry known as her *agweddi*, which was made up of a
share of all his wealth apart from land. Additionally, on the morning
after her wedding night, she was due the *cowyll*, morning-gift, also
from her husband, which amounted, essentially, to a payment for her
virginity. By contrast, the false-virgin bride was not only very likely

to be repudiated by her new husband and his kin, but by her own kin also, for having brought them shame. According to the law codes, at least, all she was due was a year-old male calf. The animal's tail was greased, and the young woman would be allowed to keep it only if she could hang onto it by the tail for a set period of time.[22]

The high value placed on female virginity had its origins mainly in economic reasons, rather than any specific religious morality. The male-dominated kin-groups wished to ensure that their property passed only to their own descendants. To ensure this, it was necessary, in early Wales as in many other cultures, to control female sexual behaviour, and, in particular, to ensure that no-one other than the *de facto* husband had sexual access to the mother of his sons. A virgin bride makes a good starting point: a non-virgin might already be carrying another man's child who might then intrude into the inheritance. Moreover, as marriage alliances were one of the ways in which social groups were formed, political ties cemented and kin-groups inter-linked, the sexual behaviour of women reflected on their entire kin. The bride was a token of alliance, a glue that was meant to bind together kin-groups. If she proved to be flawed, she dishonoured her own relatives and insulted those of her new husband. This could have very serious side effects, notably the initiation of blood-feuds. Thus, it was in the interest of kin-groups to keep their unmarried girls at home under the authority of their immediate family. This reduced the likelihood of anyone gaining sexual access to her in a manner that was not accepted by the family.[23] Wives, similarly, were considered better protected by remaining within the home environment. The public sphere was an inappropriate place for a woman, for it laid her open to possible sexual annexation by outsiders, and a woman whose sexual continence could not be guaranteed became a threat to the native system of inheritance.

This emphasis on inheritance goes part of the way to explaining the economic ramifications of a marriage. The kin of a virgin bride were transferring a valuable commodity to the kin of her husband, and helping to secure the inheritance of the husband's family. It was a major event in its consequences and various people received payment in goods or money as a result. A woman's virginity was not considered to be solely her property: far from it. The marriage brought economic advantage to her father's overlord. A virgin was considered to be in some way part of the lord's wealth: she belonged to one of his subordinates and her virginity could be used to buy an alliance which could benefit the lord. On her marriage, this potential usefulness simultaneously came into play and was ended – she had entered a new family which might then add to the lord's power-bloc, but at the same time, she could not be used again to make any further alliance. Therefore, at the marriage of a daughter, a man had to pay a fine, *amobr*, to his lord as compensation.

Women thus transferred between kin-groups, acting as a medium for social and economic exchange, as well as a physical tie providing common ground to people who might not otherwise be allies. Simultaneously, they became the vessels of alliance and inheritance – and therefore they had to be controlled. It is unclear to what extent the woman's personal feelings or preferences played any part: the law codes are not concerned with such things, and women are seldom recorded by other historical sources. In the prose tale *Branwen uerch Lyr*, the Irish king Matholwch comes to the shores of the kingdom of Bran the Blessed, the ruler of *Ynys y Kedeirn*, Britain,[24] seeking an alliance and, as part of this, requesting the hand of Bran's sister Branwen:

> First thing the next day the men of the Island of the Mighty held a council and their decision was to give Matholwch Branwen: she was one of the three great queens of the island and the most beautiful girl in the world. A time was set for the couple to sleep together.[25]

Branwen may be a queen, but from the tale it would appear that this is a position without political or personal power, and while Bran consults with all his nobility, he does not appear to have enquired of his sister her views before deciding on her marriage. Furthermore, the plot of the tale hinges upon the fact that Bran neglected to ask for the opinion and consent of his and Branwen's half-brother,

Efnissyen. Offended, the latter set in motion a chain of insult and injury which escalated ultimately into a feud between the two kingdoms. The central concern is the relationship between the two groups and the necessity of upholding good relations with allies and neighbours. Branwen herself is a function of the plot, but although the tale is named for her, it gives no space to her thoughts, feelings or reactions to the events which overtake her. What matters is the marriage, not the married woman.

A royal woman – which in the context of *Branwen* includes sisters as well as wives (and doubtless also included daughters) possessed a limited public function: like her royal male kin, she was expected to exhibit generosity and gracious behaviour to allies and to followers. But she could not dispose of her own person. Indeed, it is likely that the restrictions placed upon the movement and freedom of high-born women were greater than those of women from peasant or bond families. As a child, Nest will have seen the sisters and daughters of her father's noblemen married off at the decision of their male kin, and she will have known that this was her own future.

A woman's life was enacted essentially in private: her activities were restricted to the family and home. She was not expected to engage herself in political activity, although, if she was of high birth, her marriage could be expected to be political. The Welsh Chronicles mention women rarely, and when they do, it is almost always in the context not of a woman's own actions, but in relation to her role as it affects men. Thus Angharad ferch Maredudd is noted in the *Brutiau s. a.* 1116 not because of a deed or an action, but because she formed the physical link between two men, Gruffudd ap Llywelyn and Bleddyn ap Cynfyn – she was mother to them both in two successive marriages.[26] Similarly, Angharad ferch Owain, wife of Gruffudd ap Cynan, is noted in the same texts not just as the mother of Gruffudd's sons but as the channel which tied those sons by blood to the powerful noble family into which she had been born.[27] Where we do meet records of women acting in the public sphere in Wales in the twelfth or thirteenth centuries, they are usually not native Welsh. Rather, they are Anglo-Norman wives of Welsh noblemen or princes. For instance, in 1211, Joanna, wife of Llywelyn the Great, brokered a peace settlement between him and her father, King John – but her action is not noted by the Welsh Chronicles. Such women possessed greater freedom of action, for contemporary Anglo-Norman and Angevin society placed less emphasis upon the retention of women in a purely domestic sphere. Nest herself would benefit from this.

Under Welsh law, a man might have only one wife at a time (although this by no means precluded concubines and other extra-marital liaisons for the husband). The word used in the law codes for a wife is *gwraig*, a word which also carried the wider sense 'adult woman'. An interesting connotation arises here: the use of the same word to denote 'wife' and 'adult woman' implies that cultur-ally a woman might not be deemed completely adult if unmarried. It appears that for women, the attainment of socially recognised maturity was in part dependent on marital status as well as age. By implication, this links female adulthood with loss of virginity, and female virginity with immaturity. As female virginity was a signifi-cant part of the system for building alliances between kin-groups, and of the system for the transmission of inheritance, it becomes clear that Welsh society in this period withheld adult status from girls and women for as long as they remained in a state – virgin – where they could potentially disrupt important social rituals through unsched-uled or uncontrolled loss of that virgin state.[28]

Marriage in medieval Wales had a number of legal ramifications which differed from those found in contemporary Anglo-Norman society. In the first place, under Welsh law, a marriage did not nec-essarily have to be a lifelong contract. The first seven years of a marriage were in some ways a preliminary stage, and during them, the marriage was not yet full. In the first seven years, the spouses might legitimately separate for a number of reasons. For a woman, these were: firstly, that her husband had leprosy; or, that he was impotent; finally, that he had bad breath.[29] Moreover, if she caught him three times with another woman, she might leave and take with her all her goods.[30] Upon separation, a wife was entitled to keep her *agweddi*, the dowry equivalent due to her from her husband. The size of this was determined according to her status at birth, and was thus dependent upon her father's rank. This reference back to the birth-kin of the wife shows that during the first seven years of marriage a woman was deemed to retain some significant level of attachment to her own family. At the end of seven years, however, matters changed. Both partners retained the right to separate legally, but the wife was no longer entitled to her *agweddi*. Rather, she received a half share of all the joint property of the marriage.[31] Her status would now be calculated by reference to that of her husband, not of her blood-kin. It appears, therefore, that legally a marriage had to endure for seven years before it was considered to be fully established and fully legitimate.[32] This position differed from that of canon law, and from Anglo-Norman and Angevin practice. In the eyes of the church, all marriages were for life, with no right of separation for either party. In some senses, the Welsh practice offered a wider range of options to women, but it should be noted that we have no information as to what became of a divorced woman in Wales at that time. Her status is unlikely to have been high, and her chances of remarriage probably considerably lower than that of her ex-husband. As women were excluded from land ownership, it might have been hard for her to survive economically, unless she possessed a saleable skill, such as weaving. Many such women probably lived out their lives as servants in the houses of their kin. The divorce rules were open to abuse: they provided a means whereby a man might conveniently dispose of one spouse to make way for another who represented a new or more desirable political alliance or opportunity. Men – at least at the higher end of the social scale – often married several times, and kept concubines also. The handful of women we know of who married more than once seem to have been widows at the time of their second marriage. Nevertheless, the option of divorce must have provided the occasional chance for a woman to escape an abusive spouse and even perhaps to remarry according to her own wishes.

A woman who remained married for seven years was known as a *gwraig briod*, a wedded wife, and, alongside the separation of her legal value from that of her natal kin, she acquired new rights. During the first seven years of marriage, a woman might not enter into legally binding contracts of sale – she was not deemed to have full rights over any marital property. After seven years, she could legally buy and sell items from amongst that property. This right did not extend to land. A woman had no right to inherit land: even if her father left no other children, his land passed not to her or any sisters, or even to her or her sisters' sons, but to her father's brothers or their sons or his cousins on his father's side, or to his overlord. The sole exception was where a daughter married outside her culture: such women might transmit limited rights over land: this represents, perhaps, an adaptation by Welsh law under pressure from Anglo-Norman practice and expectations.[33] A daughter was entitled to a share of her father's moveable goods, to the value of half the amount of the same property due to her brother.[34]

At no point in her life could a medieval Welsh woman expect to be considered as fully adult in legal terms. Their status and value continued to depend upon that of the dominant man in their lives, be it father, husband, brother, son or any other. They were not defined or valued as separate individuals. Their access to law was likewise limited: the contracts of sale or exchange they might make were restricted, and any contract required the consent of her father, husband, son, or the head of her kin. Within certain fixed limits, she might make gifts: the king's wife could give away up to one third of the casual property given her by the king; the wife of an *uchelwyr* could give food, drink or clothing, and lend her household equipment. At the other end of the scale, the wife of a bondsman might give away only her head-dress and her sieve.[35]

The rules as laid down in the law codes are highly schematized and, as has been said, represent a legal ideal. In reality, it is unlikely behaviour was so strict. Nevertheless, it is clear that control of family wealth, however large or small it may be, was largely the preserve of men. Female access to it was controlled and restricted to areas which largely reflect the domestic sphere. This restriction is further restricted by the fact that, under law, a woman was never considered legally competent. She might not be a witness in a law suit, unless it be one relating to another woman. Female social and legal dependence was lifelong: a widow was valued for *sarhaed* and *galanas* in terms of her deceased husband. Doubtless in reality there were women who could and did influence the actions of husband or son or other kinsman. One example might perhaps be Cristin, one of the wives of Owain Gwynedd, son of Gruffudd ap Cynan, who was suspected of trying to influence her husband towards her sons and away from those by other wives or lovers. In principle, and probably usually in practice, however, a woman possessed no voice in the public male world, and no legal right vis a vis male actions.

It is notable that the few women we meet in prose tales who do operate in the public sphere are presented usually as generous queens who accept male norms and participate in them by assisting their dominant man in forming his political bonds, be it through obedience in marriage, or through gift-giving to allies and visitors. Thus, we are told of Branwen, after her marriage, that no visitor to her husband's court left without receiving a valuable gift from her, and that she became renowned for this behaviour, which was considered honourable for a queen.[36] When her husband shamed her, and her brothers came to her aid, she evinced little desire for revenge, but rather tried to bring about peace between the two sides, thus trying to maintain their original alliance.[37] Rhiannon possessed mystical powers, yet after she was widowed, her son Pryderi blithely offered her in marriage to his friend Manawyddan, and she accepted without demur.[38] When Rhiannon and Pryderi were magically kidnapped and the latter's wife Kigva became dependent on Manawyddan, she allowed him to make all the decisions and followed him obediently in his wanderings.[39] In opposition to these we encounter Arianrhod, who possessed considerable power, yet was repeatedly tricked or shamed by her male kin, including her exposure as a *twyllforwyn*, a false virgin.[40] It is the male who dominates.

These were the norms with which Nest grew up, and the paradigms which she must, as a child, have expected her life to follow. We cannot know what she thought of this; although, as the daughter of a king, her position was better than that of most girls, and she was probably more aware of her privilege than of the restrictions placed upon her. Her father's death and the invasions that followed must have taught her, however, how precarious the position of a woman could be. If it was her paternal uncle Rhydderch who delivered her and her brother Hywel into the hands of the Normans, this lesson may have been particularly sharp. In adulthood, she seems to have learnt the arts of persuading, perhaps even manipulating, the men around her. It may well be that she developed these skills as a response to the realisation that as a woman, she was almost wholly dependent on men.

3

NEST AND THE NORMANS

Aged probably between about seven and about twelve, Nest found herself in the power of strangers. The Norman invaders of Dyfed and Ystrad Tywi spoke French, not Welsh, dressed differently, built different types of buildings. Welsh law concerning land and land ownership centred on the kin-group. The Anglo-Normans sought to introduce new ideas of feudal tenure. Her father was dead and one of her brothers had been taken to Ireland. The other was in the prison of the man whose power was supposed to replace that of Rhys ap Tewdwr. That man was Arnulf of Montgomery.

Arnulf came from one of the most important families of Anglo-Norman England. His father, Roger of Montgomery, earl of Shrewsbury, had been one of the most trusted supporters of William the Conqueror, not only within England, but before the Conquest, in the years when the young William was struggling to impose himself over Normandy. The family had risen to prominence during the reign of William's father Duke Robert of Normandy, building themselves a package of lands in the Hiémois district. William's accession to Normandy was by no means easy: he was illegitimate, and he was a minor at the time of his father's death.[1] But the young Roger proved to be one of his most loyal and effective supporters, and reaped the rewards once William was established. In 1051, he had married Mabel de Bellême, the daughter of an important lord and landholder, William Talvas. Mabel had brothers who should rightly have succeeded to their father's lands, but one of them, Arnold, had failed in his loyalty to William, and the other, Oliver, was either unfit or declined to take the lordship. Mabel was declared her father's heiress, and her father's large estate passed, through her, to Roger, to whom she was married in 1051. The Bellême lands were not only large, they lay in a key area, on the southern border between Normandy and France, long an aggressor and a threat to the independence of the dukes. It was of great importance to William to have such lands in the hands of a man whom he might trust implicitly: Roger of Montgomery was one such. He was, through his close association with William, already one of the most influential and powerful men of the duchy. The marriage made him also one of the largest land-holders in Normandy. In 1066, he followed William to England and fought alongside him in the battle of Hastings.

As in Normandy, he again reaped the rewards of his support. William took steps to secure his new kingdom by establishing his most trusted followers in key areas. Roger was initially granted lands in Sussex, a mark of favour, but also a way of ensuring that this able and loyal man had interests in his lord's new venture. But during the first few years of his reign, William faced resistance and rebellion from the surviving Anglo-Saxon nobility. One such rebellion was that of the Shropshire landholder Eadric *Cild* in 1067, in which Eadric received the assistance of the Welsh, probably under the leadership of Bleddyn ap Cynfyn, King of Powys. Bleddyn also lent support to two further rebels, Edwin, Earl of Mercia, and Morcar, Earl of Northumbria, in 1068. William thus soon became aware of the danger to the peace of his kingdom represented by a powerful and aggressive leader in Wales.

He had already granted Herefordshire to another of his most trusted men, William fitz Osbern. In 1071, he granted Shropshire to Roger of Montgomery. The grant was pragmatic: not only was Roger loyal, he was a seasoned warrior and commander with long experience of controlling and dominating a sensitive border area. Roger brought with him into Shrewsbury trusted followers of his own, to whom he distributed lands in his new earldom. These men were to hold the territory for him, administer it, and fortify it against the Welsh.[2] A line of castles were established: these at first will have been earth and timber constructions, but would eventually turn into the great stone fortifications of Clun, Wigmore, Caux and Montgomery, amongst others. The families he introduced included the Corbets (who were by the thirteenth century to intermarry with the royal line of Powys and perhaps that of Gwynedd), and the Mortimers, who by the fourteenth century were to be a major force in English politics. In the 1070s and 1080s, the new settlers were concerned with ordering their new possessions and with beginning the process of Norman expansion into Wales. This at first proceeded slowly: William the Conqueror came to an agreement with Rhys ap Tewdwr, and baronial ambitions, particularly along the border with Shropshire and northern Herefordshire, were held in check until William's death in 1087.

Roger and his wife Mabel had nine children, five sons and four daughters, all of whom had to be provided for.[3] The eldest son, Robert (known as Robert de Bellême after his mother's family) would inherit the family's Norman holdings, and the second, Hugh, the lands in England, but that left three more sons, as well as daughters requiring dowries. Roger was wealthy and powerful, but, like other lords of that period, he did not wish to break up his lands by dividing them amongst his various heirs. To do so would not serve the long-term interests of the family. He succeeded in arranging a valuable marriage for his third son, Roger, with the heiress to the Norman comté of La Marche. But on the death of Rhys ap Tewdwr in 1093, Roger still had to provide for his sons Philip and Arnulf. As it transpired, Philip was to make no impact: he seems never to have held any lands or interests in England or Wales, and eventually died on crusade. Arnulf was another matter.

Roger's loyalty to William the Conqueror was unshakeable, but on William's death, he clearly had reservations about the new king, William Rufus. Perhaps Roger felt that Normandy and England should be retained as a single bloc; perhaps he felt some personal dislike of William Rufus, or affection for his brother Robert Curthose.[4] Whatever his reason, in 1088, he and his sons joined the rebellion against Rufus. It might have proved disastrous: in principle, he risked total dispossession, imprisonment, and even death. But in practice, he survived unscathed. Perhaps William Rufus recognised his value, perhaps Roger was simply too big and too influential to remove. For Roger, the rebellion proved rewarding: William remained king, yes, but he permitted the border lords to break the old agreement with Rhys ap Tewdwr and to resume their colonial activities in Wales.

Roger may well have been uncomfortably aware of develop-ments to the north of his Shropshire lands. William the Conqueror had had no agreement with any king of, or claimant to, Gwynedd, and as a result the Earl of Chester, Hugh d'Avranches, and his vassal Robert of Rhuddlan had made considerable gains in north Wales. The imprisonment of Gruffudd ap Cynan and the relative youth of the heirs of Trahaearn ap Caradog left Robert with relatively little opposition, and his influence spread deep into Wales, perhaps even as far as Anglesey, from his stronghold at the former north Welsh royal site at Rhuddlan. With his sons to provide for, and with an eye on his own wealth and influence, Roger perhaps viewed this success with caution. With the death of William the Conqueror, his voice at the English court was eclipsed by the intimates of William Rufus. It is likely he did not wish to be overtaken or overwhelmed by a power-ful neighbour.

Bernard of Neufmarché, the conqueror of Brycheiniog and the man who had brought about the death of Rhys ap Tewdwr, does not seem to have owed his position in the borders to Roger. Rather, he probably owed his Herefordshire lands to William the Conqueror or one of his representatives in that area. But he seems to have been on fair terms with the family of Montgomery, and Roger made no objection to Bernard's advance into mid-Wales. In light of its sequel, indeed, one wonders if there was a degree of collaboration – or at least advance planning – between the two. Bernard remained in the east, while Roger, with his sons Robert, Hugh and Arnulf, pursued the new Norman advantage in Wales into the south-west.

The family and its dependent barons had made limited advances into Wales since 1071: at Clun, for example, one of Roger's vassals from his homeland of the Hiémois, Picot de Saï, had penetrated west into Welsh upland territory, perhaps starting from the area around Caux. By 1086, Robert's sheriff in Shropshire, Rainault, was collecting the annual renders from two Welsh commots as well as his Shropshire lands. Montgomery Castle itself lay in land which may have been Welsh: it is listed in *Domesday Book* as having been waste in 1066, raising the possibility that it may have been part of the debatable land fought over in the 1050s by Gruffudd ap Llywelyn and the Anglo-Saxons.[5] In its hinterland, Roger and his men established a line of earthwork fortifications extending as far as Llandinam.[6] These advances doubtless brought Roger or his representatives into contact with the Welsh, and not only the farmers and local lords of the lands they annexed, but the overlords, who must have included the sons of Bleddyn ap Cynfyn. We know of no certain contact between any of the sons of Bleddyn and any member of Roger's family before 1102, but in that year, they are found collaborating. It was, as will be seen, probably an alliance of convenience: the interests of the two groups were at odds. Yet some sort of relationship between the two must have been necessary before this time, if only to reduce the dangers of raids, counter-raids, ambushes and conflicts along their borders.[7] In 1093, when Rhys ap Tewdwr was killed, Cadwgan ab Bleddyn probably had a keen idea as to what his eastern neighbour the Earl of Shrewsbury was likely to do, and this may have precipitated his own rapid invasion of Deheubarth, in the hope of establishing himself in at least part of that land before Roger and his forces could arrive.[8]

We do not know the exact route taken into Wales by Roger and his army, but it is likely to have begun with the wide sweep of the Severn valley, pushing west through the old kingdom of Buellt and perhaps through parts of the lands of the sons of Bleddyn. With this advance, they established defensive positions, including what would become Cardigan, Pembroke and Carmarthen. Around the same time, Bernard of Neufmarché continued his own advance westwards down the Usk valley, likewise building castles, which included

Bronllys, Crickhowell and Tretower. His armies were to arrive in Deheubarth by 1095, in which year they ravaged Gower and Cydweli. It must have seemed to the west Welsh that they were being battered by wave after wave of relentless would-be conquerors.

They fought back: we have already seen how Gerald the Constable found himself besieged at Pembroke, and in 1094 the Normans found themselves temporarily driven back from all their new castles save Pembroke and Carmarthen. But they continued to pressure the Welsh. Roger of Montgomery died in 1094, but this did not lead to any decrease of Norman activity. His sons, notably Hugh and Arnulf, continued to advance and to fight. Hugh was now Earl of Shrewsbury, and followed his father's initiative to establish a new lordship for Arnulf. He was to devote most of his life to the fight to increase Norman settlement in Wales.

Perhaps as early as the end of 1093, Arnulf seems to have considered himself as the new lord of Pembroke, looking to hold the valuable agricultural lands of the old kingdom of Dyfed. To his east, Carmarthen became the main Welsh fortress of William fitz Baldwin, William Rufus's sheriff of Devon. Beyond William, the area around Llandovery became the lordship of another family, the Cliffords.

What was Arnulf like? He was a member of a well-known and politically important family, but he is less well recorded than his elder brothers, Robert, Hugh and Roger. The Anglo-Norman historian, Orderic Vitalis, described his father, Roger of Montgomery, as 'a wise and prudent man, a lover of justice, who always enjoyed the company of sober and learned men.'[9] One of these 'learned men' was Odelerius, Orderic's father: Orderic thus had had access to direct information on Roger and his sons. But he does not tell us very much about Arnulf, and his feelings about the entire family were mixed. Mabel de Bellême he excoriated for her rapacious attitude to church lands in Normandy and especially those of Saint-Évroul, and, perhaps, for her unfashionably forceful personality: he calls her 'that cruel woman, who had shed the blood of many and had forcibly disinherited many lords'.[10] He had few good words to say for her eldest son Robert, either, as we shall see. As far as Arnulf was concerned, he was ambivalent:

However Roger [Roger of Montgomery's third son] and Arnulf, who were much regarded among their companions for their knightly skill and reputation for valour, married highly-born wives through their father's advice and their own efforts. Both throve for a while with comital rank, enjoying power and wealth, but before their deaths they lost by treachery the honours they had won.[11]

This tells us more about the times than it does about Arnulf personally. He had been born at a time and into a class in which male prowess at arms was highly regarded and in which the only careers open to the younger sons of the nobility were the church or warfare and colonisation. Two of his brothers entered the church (Philip and the half-brother Everard), but Arnulf perhaps was not suited to or interested in such a life. We should perhaps imagine him as something of a pragmatist: a tough, military-minded man, loyal where he chose and was rewarded, but probably capable of ruthlessness where required, and self-interested in most circumstances. Sensitivity, altruism and soft-heartedness were not survival characteristics in the world he inhabited. To support himself, he needed land, or a wealthy patron, or both. After the death of William the Conqueror, the sympathies of the Montgomery family tended to lie not with the new king of England, William Rufus, but with Robert Curthose in Normandy. Normandy, however, did not provide much opportunity to landless younger sons by this period. To Arnulf, Wales must have seemed like his best chance. We do not know exactly how much time he devoted to the conquest of Dyfed in person – he seems to have come and gone. However, just as his father had brought his Norman followers to settle in Shropshire, so Arnulf persuaded his own friends and followers to come with him to Dyfed. That there were men to follow him, a landless younger son, tells us both something about his personal charisma and influence, and about the land-hungriness of these lesser Normans, mostly themselves landless younger sons. These may have included the founders of the families of de Barri, de Brian, fitz Wizo, fitz Martin and fitz Tancard.[12] Chief amongst these was Gerald, known usually as Gerald of Windsor, whom we have already met as the clever defender of Pembroke castle.

Gerald was to become one of the most important figures in Nest's life, and a significant one in the conquest of south Wales. Yet we know very little about his origins. His father supposedly was one of the stewards to William the Conqueror at Windsor: he belonged, thus, to the lower section of the nobility, and, prior to his appearance in Wales, seems not to have held any lands of his own. He must have met Arnulf or Roger of Montgomery at the royal court and become one of their men, perhaps at first in a relatively low position. It seems that he pleased them – or Arnulf, at least – and they trusted him, for Arnulf installed him as steward and castellan of the new castle at Pembroke, intended to be the centre of Arnulf's new lordship. From Gerald's point of view, this was a highly desirable position. If he carried out his duties well, and pleased his new lord, he could hope to be rewarded with lands of his own and in time to rise to a position of considerable influence within south-west Wales. He must, by 1093, have had some military experience, to be entrusted with such a role. We should imagine him in the Montgomery forces fighting in the Welsh borders. He was also, it would appear from his career, a clever man, and one who knew where his advantage lay. From 1093 he was based in Wales and it is not impossible that he learnt to speak Welsh. Certainly, he must have acquainted himself with Welsh customs, laws and practices. In time, under Henry I, he would have to administer law in the lordship of Pembroke.

I have suggested in Chapter Two that Nest fell into the hands of Arnulf or his men probably less than a year after her father's death. They were not psychopaths, nor is it likely that they set out to be deliberately cruel or sadistic. But they were career warriors. To them, Nest was less a child to be protected or rescued, than a prize of war. It is unlikely she was severely mistreated, but the experience of capture must nevertheless have been terrifying. She would have become accustomed to warriors in her father's halls, but those were his personal warband, to whom she was the king's daughter, to be respected, perhaps even indulged. The Normans were something new. It is likely that Arnulf's forces included translators, probably men of Anglo-Welsh blood from the borderlands of Shropshire and Powys. But the bulk of his followers spoke French or English, dressed differently to the Welsh and followed different customs. A girl of lower birth would probably have faced rape or rough handling. Nest's royal blood is likely to have protected her from that, particularly if she was handed over formally by a kinsman or by one of the Welsh noblemen of Dyfed. We do not know if her mother was with her. It may be that after her capture, Nest never saw her again. Alternatively, they may have been captured together. There is no way, now, of telling. Nest was of far more value to her captors than her mother, and it is likely that Arnulf or his representative – quite possibly Gerald – decided to separate them. Nest was still young enough to be educated and introduced to Norman customs; and, as a virgin, she was of value as a potential bride for someone. She may also have been notably pretty – as an adult, her beauty was to be famous. The land rights of the widowed Gwladus were far less clear, and she may have been thought old.

While we possess no evidence as to how Nest was viewed and treated by the new Norman lord of Dyfed and his men, we do possess a reasonable amount of information about Norman attitudes to heiresses in general, and about the way in which other such girls were treated. Under Welsh law – and, perhaps, in her own eyes – Nest possessed no claim over her father's kingdom. The Normans, as we will see, took a different view.

The Normans have received a bad press for their attitudes to women: they have been blamed for both a degradation of female rights in England, and, more recently, in the Celtic-speaking countries.[13] In both cases, this judgement was based in rather particular pre-conceptions about the status of women in England, Wales or Ireland in the pre-Norman period, and, indeed, in pre-conceptions about their native cultures, Anglo-Saxon or 'Celtic' and, indeed, about those cultures themselves.[14] As Pauline Stafford has shown, for the case of England, the realities were somewhat different. For Wales, Professor Wendy Davies has gone some way to re-assessing the position of women, but more work is needed.[15] In 1093, Nest stood poised between two worlds: that of her Welsh blood, and that of her new overlords. To understand her, we need to understand how those new lords viewed women, what they expected of them, and what part they played in the important system of the transmission and inheritance of land, goods and status.

When he was crowned in Westminster Abbey on 5 August 1100, the new King Henry I issued a coronation charter, addressing the various issues which had occupied his new subjects during the reign of his predecessor, William Rufus – and in particular the rights of the clergy, of noble men and of noble women. The clauses relating specifically to women read as follows:

> If any of my barons or of my tenants shall wish to give in marriage his daughter or his sister or his niece or his cousin, he shall consult me about the matter; but I will neither seek payment for my consent, nor will I refuse my permission, unless he wishes to give her in marriage to one of my enemies. And if, on the death of one of my barons or of one of my tenants, a daughter should be his heir, I will dispose of her in marriage and of her lands according to the counsel given me by my barons. And if the wife of one of my tenants shall survive her husband and be without children, she shall have her dower and her marriage portion, and I will not give her in marriage unless she herself consents. If a widow survives with children under age, she shall have her dower and her marriage portion, so long as she keeps her body chaste; and I will not give her in marriage except with her consent. And the guardian of the land, and of the children, shall be either the widow or another of their relations, as may seem more proper. And I order that my barons shall act likewise towards the sons and daughters and widows of their men.[16]

The concerns this reveals are very much those we have already met in the context of medieval Welsh law: the proper control and transmission of property and land; the rights of men over their kinswomen; and the rights of women over the goods or rights granted to them on marriage. It is not, of course, a definitive statement on the rights and status of women in Anglo-Norman England at the dawn of the twelfth century. The charter is concerned with property rights, and thus with the interests of the upper social classes. The issues of the education of women, their permitted spheres of activity, their access to work, the expectations placed upon their behaviour and the opportunities offered to them are not germane here, and are either omitted or only touched upon obliquely. The situation of women of the non-land-holding classes is not addressed at all. But what Henry's coronation charter does tell us about is the aspects about women that were of particular importance to the leading men of his kingdom – the matters that he had to consider in order to secure their support and approval.[17]

Unlike in Wales, in Anglo-Norman eyes a woman could inherit land, and as the charter demonstrates, the question of heiresses was an important one. As Eleanor Searle has shown, heiresses provided an important conduit by which legitimate title to and control over land might be transmitted, not simply from generation to generation, but from conquered to conqueror.[18] Henry himself married partly for reasons of legitimisation. England belonged to the Norman kings by right of conquest, but the old blood-line of the Anglo-Saxon kings still survived and had intermarried with that of the kings of Scotland. Henry chose to marry a daughter of the Scottish king, Edith-Matilda, at least in part to further legitimise his own kingship.[19]

Nest was the daughter of the last reigning king of Deheubarth. In the eyes of her Welsh compatriots, she possessed no rights to the kingdom, nor might she pass any claim to it to a husband. But the Normans did not see it in these terms, and, having begun the process of colonisation, most probably intended to apply the laws of their own culture to their new lands. To them, Nest was a potential heiress and control of her and her marriage could prove lucrative.

Of course, she had brothers and, in both Welsh and Norman eyes, the right to succeed to Rhys ap Tewdwr belonged in theory to them. However, under Norman feudal practice, a son's right to inherit might be ignored or removed in certain circumstances – or if it proved convenient. This had been the case with Roger of Montgomery's wife Mabel de Bellême. Her brother Arnold was set aside from the succession in her favour on the grounds that he had proved disloyal to his overlord, Duke William (later William the Conqueror).[20] This not only allowed William to undermine an enemy, it permitted him to reward and elevate one of his own most loyal followers. It is very likely that in Nest's case, it will have occurred to her captors that she might be used in just such a way. Her brothers could be – and, in the long run were – excluded from possession of Dyfed and Ystrad Tywi on the grounds of being the children of enemies and potential enemies themselves. Nest was a very valuable prize indeed.

To the Normans, as to the Welsh, women as conduits of inheritance required control, and their marriages and chastity were thus of great importance. But Norman attitudes to women differed from those of Wales in certain other ways. In particular, Welsh culture allowed no place to women as political beings: we have no trace, even in the prose tales, of women as regents or as positive influences on public life.[21] While the power of women in Anglo-Norman England was still limited, and considerably less than that of men, certain very high status women were able to exercise influence in the political sphere.[22] William I's queen, Matilda, exercised considerable powers in both Normandy and England during her husband's absences and seems to have enjoyed a high degree of confidence from her husband. But it does appear that women under the Anglo-Normans had a rather wider pool of rights than those in Wales. One area in which this is particularly visible is that of religion. We find a fair number of women founding churches or granting property to them: this would have been unthinkable in Wales. There was no tradition in eleventh-century Wales of kings or nobles endowing monasteries, and we possess no reliable evidence on the nature and expression of lay piety at that time. In contrast, piety seems to have been one of the virtues expected of Anglo-Norman women. For example, Judith, William the Conqueror's niece, founded a nunnery at Elstow in 1076 – she was a widow, and was disposing of her lands without husbandly consent or interference.[23] We find other women praised for their faith; however, it should be noted in passing that this to some extent is due to the nature of our surviving sources. These were written, by and large, by monks or clerics, and reflect the val-

ues, interests and expectations of such men. The Canterbury monk
Eadmer wrote of Edith-Matilda:

> ...no earthly concerns, no pageantry of this world's glory could keep her
> from going on before to the different places to which Anselm was coming;
> and, as the monks and canons went out as usual to meet the Archbishop,
> she went on ahead and by her careful forethought saw to it that his vari-
> ous lodgings were richly supplied with suitable furnishings.[24]

It was, in the eyes of such men, the duty of women to show respect
and duty to the church. The pictures they give us are designed not
simply to inform but to teach: they are supplying images of 'good'
and 'bad' female (and male) behaviour. Some of the venom displayed
by Orderic Vitalis in his account of Mabel de Bellême is due to the
fact that she was acquisitive, rather than generous, in her relations
with the church. It is clear that, as in Wales, a woman was expected
to conform to certain norms of behaviour. In many ways, they were
probably similar.

NEST THE CAPTIVE

What became of Nest after she came into the hands of the Normans?
We do not know; as with so much of her life, we can only speculate. Her brother Hywel, it appears, remained imprisoned, perhaps at
Pembroke, which was to prove the strongest of all the Norman castles
in Wales, perhaps at another of the strongholds of the Montgomery
family.[25] In such a place, he was under the eyes of those most directly
concerned with controlling and colonising Deheubarth, and might
be publicly disposed of, should he ever become a focus for rebellion.
In the case of Nest, however, it is likely that she was removed from
her homeland.

There are a number of reasons for this. In the first instance, the early
Norman settlement was essentially military in character, made up
of fortified encampments of men, with little or no female presence.

Those few women who may have been within the camps were probably not considered fit companions for the daughter of a fallen king and a potential heiress. And then, Welsh reaction to the invasion was swift and aggressive. Armed resistance began in 1094 and continued throughout the 1090s. The leader of this was Cadwgan ab Bleddyn, the man who had invaded Deheubarth in 1088 and 1093. From 1094, Cadwgan and his associates brought warfare to almost every part of Wales.[26] It seems that the killing of Rhys ap Tewdwr had provided the impetus needed to inspire the leading men to violent action. Cadwgan's motives were probably more to do with personal ambition than national feeling: the removal of Rhys presented him with an opportunity to attempt to enhance his own power and impose his influence on a wider stage. The death of Roger of Montgomery in 1094 and the involvement of at least some of the latter's forces in Deheubarth, moreover, removed one check on Cadwgan's behaviour. His Norman neighbours were distracted, and this allowed him to begin his campaign to establish himself not only in Powys but in the wider Welsh polity also. In 1094, he struck north, into Gwynedd, once ruled by his father Bleddyn. By 1096, matters had escalated to the point where William Rufus became involved, bringing an army against the rebels. But they eluded him, sacking Montgomery itself, storming and seizing the castle at Carmarthen and inflicting a defeat upon the Normans in Brycheiniog. Cadwgan, by now joined by his cousin, Uchdryd ab Edwin, lord of Tegeingl and one of the most powerful of the nobility of Gwynedd, and by Hywel ap Goronwy, one of the *uchelwyr* of Buellt, attacked Pembroke castle and plundered the land around it. It was as close as Arnulf was to come to losing his new lordship. In the north, Earl Hugh of Chester released Gruffudd ap Cynan from prison, in the hope of splitting the loyalties of the northern Welsh, and seems to have found some way to suborn Uchdryd ab Edwin and his brother Owain away from Cadwgan. By 1098, Cadwgan, with Gruffudd ap Cynan, who had joined him, was under pressure, besieged upon Anglesey by the joint forces of Earl Hugh of Chester and of Arnulf's brother, Earl Hugh of Shrewsbury.

It is hard to know what the outcome of this siege might have been

1 Pembroke Castle

2 Cilgerrran Castle

Left: 3 Stone keep typical of the early Norman period (Hedingham Castle)

Below: 4 St David's Cathedral, where Nest's son David was bishop

5 (Detail) Decorated initial showing William the Conqueror

6 (Detail) Imaginary portrait of King William II

7 (RH miniature) King Henry I seated on his throne

8 Gerald of Wales

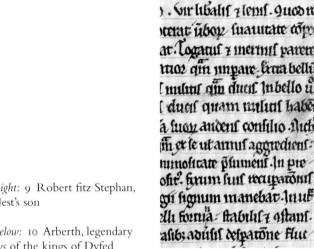

Right: 9 Robert fitz Stephan, Nest's son

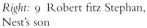

Below: 10 Arberth, legendary *llys* of the kings of Dyfed

Above left: 11 Robert de Bellême's fortress at Bridgenorth

Above right: 12 Bronyllys Castle

Below: 13 Cardigan Castle, home of Stephen of Cardigan

Right: 14 Carew Castle, established by Gerald of Windsor

Below: 15 The Corbet Castle of Caux

16 Cilgerrran Castle, scene of Nest's abduction

17 Dinefwr, traditional seat of the kings of Deheubarth

18 Kidwelly Castle

19 Laugharne Castle

20 Llanamdyffri Castle

21 Llanstephan Castle, held by Nest's son Maurice

22 Manorbier, birthplace of Gerald of Wales

23 Pembroke Castle

Right: 24 Pillar ar Carew commemorating Nest's kinsman Maredudd ab Edwin

Below: 25 The Maredudd ap Edwin Inscription

Left: 26 Shrewsbury Castle

Below: 27 Robert de Bellême's castle at Tickhill

Right: 28 Tretower Castle

Below: 29 Wigmore Castle

30 Llawhaden, a palace of the bishops of St Davids

31 Carreg Cennan castle, founded perhaps by Nest's nephew, the Lord Rhys

32 Crickhowell Castle

33 Clun Castle

34 Montgomery Castle

Above: 35 Norman wooden castle (reconstruction at Stansted Montfichet)

Left: 36 Norman arch, Brecon

had the two sides committed to battle. The Welsh were almost certainly outnumbered, and the chances of either Cadwgan or Gruffudd
– or both – being killed would have been high. Had such a thing
come to pass, the history of Wales in the twelfth and thirteenth centuries would have been dramatically different: indeed, the conquest
of the entire country might have been achieved nearly two hundred
years earlier. In the event, however, battle was prevented by what
can only be described as an accident of history. The king of Norway,
Magnus Bareleg, was in the Irish Sea with his fleet, seeking to impose
his authority upon the Viking colonies of the Western Isles and the
Isle of Man. He, or one of his men, sighted the army drawn up on
the Welsh coast, and came closer to investigate. Someone, either from
within the fleet, or from the Norman army, opened archery fire:
the other side retaliated. In the ensuing confused combat, Hugh of
Shrewsbury was shot and killed. His ally Hugh of Chester and their
forces withdrew, and, as they retreated back through north Wales,
Owain ab Edwin, who had previously assisted them, turned on
them. It was an unexpected setback for the Normans, and a lucky
chance for Cadwgan and Gruffudd who, wary of what would happen when the Normans re-grouped, and also probably of Owain
ab Edwin, who was showing a talent for changing sides, fled to
Ireland.

The Anglesey incident marked the end of the 1090s rebellion. It
was by now in the interests of both sides to come to terms. Peace
was made, and the two Welsh leaders, Cadwgan and Gruffudd, had at
least some parts of the lands they had sought granted to them. Over
the next twenty to thirty years both were to adopt policies of slow
but steady expansion outwards.

It is very probable that Nest was sent out of Wales during this
period, if only to prevent her being seized and married off to one of
the Welsh rebels. The most likely place for her to have been sent, at
least at first, was to somewhere within the English lands of Arnulf or
his brothers, perhaps in the care of one of their trusted vassal families.
We cannot know for certain where, however.

There are no very direct parallels with which to compare Nest's situation. In the wake of the Norman Conquest of England, a number of women – widows, sisters, daughters, nieces – took refuge in convents, or were placed in them by their male kin for safety.[27] In the case of heiresses, this practice seems to have continued, at least in certain circumstances, on through the eleventh century. The most famous case is that of Edith-Matilda, the future wife of Henry I, who was sent to a convent, perhaps for education, by her father, Malcolm of Scotland.[28] As both the daughter of a king and as a descendant of the old Anglo-Saxon royal line, she was a significant person, and the English king – by then William Rufus – took an interest in her marriage. Placing her in a convent was probably also a strategy by her family to protect her against the designs of would-be spouses – and perhaps to reduce the chances of interference from the king of England. In the event, William succeeded in thwarting a plan to marry her to the lord of Richmond, Alan, who, as a son-in-law, would have been too useful an ally to Malcolm. A convent was not a hundred per cent secure, however, and, baulked of Edith-Matilda, Alan carried off another heiress-refugee, Gunnilda, daughter of King Harold Godwinesson, who had died at Hastings. She had claim on a considerable bloc of territory.[29] Such heiresses were highly desirable, but they were also dangerous. Marriage to one of them could bring a lord not only wealth but considerable influence: it was of great importance to the king of England to keep control over what became of them, and to ensure that only loyal men were able to marry them. This, indeed, is part of the point of the clauses in Henry I's coronation charter.[30] Nest, viewed in this light, presented a possible danger to the stability of royal control over Norman colonies and lords in south-west Wales.

While Roger of Montgomery had proved himself completely loyal to William the Conqueror, William Rufus could never be sure either of him or of his sons. Hugh and Arnulf, at least, held lands of him, yet both, along with their Norman-based brothers Robert and Roger, showed a tendency to prefer his elder brother Robert, duke of Normandy. It is entirely possible that, upon gaining control of Nest, Arnulf may have considered her as a potential wife for himself. William Rufus would not have looked favourably upon such a notion. In the 1090s, the idea of the quasi-independent, militaristic 'Marcher Lord' had not yet really arisen, but its origins were already in place. In later centuries, English kings were to face problems with influential, wealthy lords with lands in Wales and its borders who had succeeded in obtaining for themselves a series of almost-royal powers over their lands, and who denied aspects of royal authority over them.[31] These would include two families introduced by Roger of Montgomery – the Corbets of Caux and the Mortimers. In the later twelfth century, indeed, one lord – Richard de Clare, known as Strongbow – was to marry a daughter of an Irish king, and through her inherit what was essentially an independent kingdom.[32] The attempts of the first three Norman kings to control the marriages of their nobility were in part designed to prevent this sort of thing from happening. At the other end of the Anglo-Norman, Angevin and Plantagenet expansion into Wales, Edward I was to ensure that the last members of the royal line of Gwynedd – the daughter of Llywelyn the Last, and the daughters and sons of his younger brother Dafydd – were placed out of the reach of ambitious barons. The boys lived out their lives in captivity; the girls were placed in convents far away from Wales and professed from an early age as nuns.[33]

It is possible that Nest, too, may have found herself placed for a while, in a convent: it would have been seen as a safe and appropriate place for a young girl who was, probably, below the age for marriage. If so, she might have received some level of education, certainly on religion, perhaps also in reading and writing, and the kinds of arithmetic useful to the chatelaine of a manor or a castle. Another possibility is that she might have been placed in a foster family, perhaps amongst the followers of the Montgomery family. If this did occur, one might make a case for this having been the Corbets of Longdon and Alcester. This was probably a junior branch of the family established at Caux by Roger of Montgomery.[34] We know that Robert Corbet, the baron of Longdon and Alcester, had two daughters, at least one of whom, Sybil, may have been around the same age as Nest or a little older. Sybil, with her sister Alice, was herself an heiress, as her father seems to have had no sons (or if so, they predeceased him). Sybil was to marry Herbert fitz Herbert, son of a royal chamberlain, but before this she was one of the mistresses of Henry I, with whom she had a son, Rainald, who was alive and adult in 1130.[35] Nest was also to become one of Henry's mistresses. We do not know when she met Henry, or under what circumstances, but one possible context would be if she had had some connexion with Sybil Corbet. One advantage of placing Nest with such a family was that, settled as they were in a border shire, they might have had Welsh-speaking servants, or, at least, been able to hire a Welsh-speaking maid to assist the new captive. Wherever she was sent, Nest must have found herself expected to learn Norman French: a family with young daughters would be geared to provide for her other needs. The rhythm of life in a small baronial household would in certain ways have mimicked that which she had experienced in Wales. Activities will have centred around the agricultural cycles and the official duties of the lord in administering his lands. He would also have had obligations to his overlord: there would, perhaps, have been visits to the castles or strongholds of Earl Hugh of Shrewsbury, to market centres and to churches or monasteries. The concerns of female life, too, will have seemed similar: the production and maintenance of clothing; embroidery; the overseeing of food production and household duties. Nest would have participated in such lessons as a household chaplain might have given to the Corbet daughters. With a family such as the Corbets of Longdon and Alcester, Nest might even have helped out with harvests. In other ways, the household must have seemed very alien. There were the obvious differences in language and in dress and hair-styling, but there would also have been more subtle ones of custom and behaviour. Robert Corbet would not have had a *teulu*, an aristocratic warband whom he was obliged to feast and reward with gifts on a regular basis. His estate was small, and though he undoubtedly travelled around it, his daughters – and Nest, if she was with them – may have remained mainly at one place. This would have been a great change away from Nest's childhood, travelling all over Deheubarth with her royal father and his full household. The type of visitors that came to a man like Robert Corbet would have differed, too: not great aristocrats or Viking merchants, but the lesser figures of neighbours or travelling craftsmen. Would Robert and his daughters have visited Earl Hugh at Montgomery or in Shrewsbury? Perhaps, but it seems unlikely in such unsettled times.

Against this possibility, it must be said that Robert Corbet of Longdon and Alcester does not seem to have been one of the more trusted or closer followers of Roger of Montgomery or his sons. It was his elder brother, Roger Corbet of Caux, who is found working closely with them.[36] A minor vassal might not have seemed an appropriate guardian for Nest, in Arnulf's eyes – or, indeed, a competent one. Shropshire and the neighbouring Montgomery lands were not necessarily safe from the Welsh, as was demonstrated by the attack on Montgomery in 1096. By then, Arnulf had English lands of his own, in Holderness and Lincolnshire.[37] He might have entrusted Nest to a family based there.

It must have been around this time that Nest first encountered a stone building that was not religious in function. The Welsh kings of the eleventh and earlier centuries built in wood, not stone, and their halls, as has been seen, were conglomerations of separate buildings, rather than multi-chambered or multi-storey. The impact of even a small early stone keep upon her was probably considerable. In later years, the stone castle proved a powerful and tangible symbol of not only the presence of the Normans and Angevins but also their strength, their wealth, and their determination to stay. It seems cliché, but to a child or young woman, such buildings were very likely a cause for wonder.

Yet another possibility as to what became of Nest is that Arnulf was at some point obliged to surrender her to the king. The Montgomery brothers seem to have involved themselves in further agitation against William Rufus in 1095.[38] William put the conspiracy down around the time of the destruction of Montgomery by the Welsh, and the latter event brought him to Wales. He aided Earl Hugh – despite the latter's spotty record of loyalty – but he might well have learnt of Nest at this time, and perhaps elected to take control of her before she was married off to Arnulf or one of his major followers within south-west Wales. The marriage of Arnulf of Montgomery, a member of one of the greatest noble families of England and Normandy, was not a minor matter, and such marriages intimately involved the king. A loyal nobleman – like Arnulf's father Roger of Montgomery – might be rewarded with a great heiress as wife, but to do so involved a high level of trust. With wide lands came not only wide responsibility, but also large resources and considerable power. Such lords possessed many tenants and vassals of their own, upon whom they might call. If their lands lay in border or other sensitive zones, they might become significant players in the political sphere, bartering their support to rival rulers in return for personal gain. The gift of Mabel de Bellême and her lands to Roger of Montgomery had come back to haunt the kings of England and dukes of Normandy in the second generation. Roger's sons – especially the eldest, Robert – proved themselves to be ambitious, self-interested and unreliable. It is very hard to imagine that William Rufus would have willingly seen Arnulf married to a girl through whom he might advance a claim to the whole of the old kingdom of Deheubarth. Arnulf's new lordship of Pembroke was already significant: easily re-provisioned by sea, it could easily provide a rebellious lord with a base of operations which would be hard for his putative overlord to attack effectively. It opened up the possibility of communication behind the king's back with Normandy and Ireland. It was a situation that required royal monitoring. Neither Arnulf nor his brother Hugh, Earl of Shrewsbury, belonged to William's inner circle, and were very seldom at his court. Given their track-record, William must have worried, at least intermittently, what exactly they were doing or planning.

Arnulf is unlikely to have surrendered Nest voluntarily, nor did he see William Rufus on a regular basis. Indeed, he was in Normandy at least some of the time, leaving men such as Gerald of Windsor to hold, defend and increase his holdings in south-west Wales. He could not, however, have concealed his possession of Nest for long. We know that the lord who was engaged in the conquest of Gwent and

Glamorgan was Robert fitz Hamo, a close friend and supporter of the king. Moreover, William Rufus came in person to Wales and its borders at least twice.

His first visit occurred in the autumn of 1095, and he came with an army. He was responding to the Welsh uprising which had begun in 1094 and had resulted already in widespread destruction. William almost certainly hoped to quash it, and to force the Welsh leaders to come to terms. Perhaps, too, he hoped to enforce awareness of his own military prowess upon his own border lords. However, the expedition brought him no advantage: he failed to encounter any of the Welsh leaders in battle, or to capture or retake any strongholds. Instead, the Welsh chose to retreat into the uplands and the forests, evading him in what was to become a familiar strategy to successive kings of England.

To which part of Wales did he come? The E-Text of the *Anglo-Saxon Chronicle* tells us that he came in response to the fall of Montgomery castle.[39] 'And his army divided and went through all that land, until on All Saints' [1 November] the army came together to Snowdon.'[40] Travelling between the diverse areas of Wales in the medieval period was never the easiest of tasks, and the weather and oncoming winter cannot have made it easier for William and his men. We may doubt that he did, in fact, travel all over Wales: he may have restricted his activities to the old kingdom of Powys and the uplands of Gwynedd.[41] This is where we would expect to find Cadwgan ab Bleddyn, leader of the Welsh resistance, and his allies. It is very likely, however, that William met with Earl Hugh at this time, and came to know of the capture of Nest. Did he take charge of her in autumn 1095? We do not know. Leaving Wales, he went north, to Northumberland, where he was engaged in putting down the rebellion of Robert Mowbray, earl of that area. It would seem unlikely that he would take a young female captive with him on such an activity, but he might quite easily have ordered her to be escorted to the place of his choice. We might well imagine Nest being passed from place to place and hand to hand several times in the two years after her father's death. William returned to Wales with an army in the summer of 1097, and once again found himself thwarted. It was his last visit that we know of: upon withdrawing, the *Anglo-Saxon Chronicle* (E) tells us that he ordered the construction of fortifications along the borders of Norman territories within Wales. He did not, however, put an end to Norman expansion or aggression within Wales, and, as we have seen, the warfare continued on down to 1099.

Perhaps, though we cannot know for certain, Nest was now a royal ward. We do not know if the king had taken charge of her or where she was. It is not impossible that she was taken to the royal court, perhaps to keep her out of the reach of ambitious barons. As with so much in her early life, we have only speculation.

We do know that at some time in her life, she encountered William Rufus' brother Henry. We know that she had his child. There are two periods in her life when this is more likely to have happened. One, as will be discussed later, is the years around 1108–1115. The other is in these lost years between her father's death in 1093 and her marriage, which, as will be seen, probably occurred around 1102.

NEST AND HENRY: A COURT ROMANCE?

For Nest to have encountered Henry before he became king in 1100, we must suppose that she had indeed become a royal ward or captive, and that she was taken at some point away from Wales and the Marches to one of the courts or estates of William Rufus. She possessed no relatives in England to whom she might be entrusted, barring her tenuous relationship to the wife of Bernard of Neufmarché, another Nest.[42] But Bernard was himself a Marcher lord, like Hugh of Shrewsbury and his brother Arnulf, and had been implicated in the rebellion against William in 1088. He was also responsible for the death of Nest's father. We probably should not suppose that he became Nest's guardian.

The Anglo-Norman court would have been a completely new world to Nest, who, in the second part of the 1090s, must have been aged somewhere between about ten and about fifteen. That she was more than twelve is likely in this scenario: a child would probably have been fostered, but at twelve and above she was of marriageable age.

What was the Anglo-Norman court like under William Rufus? The monkish writers thought badly of it. Orderic wrote that the courtiers and noblemen:

> ...rejected the traditions of honest men, ridiculed the counsel of priests, and persisted in their barbarous style of dress ... Some of them frivolled away their time, spending it as they chose without regard for the law of God or the customs of their ancestors. They devoted their nights to feast and drinking-bouts, idle chatter, dice, games of chance and other sports and they slept all day ... Our wanton youth is sunk in effeminacy and courtiers, fawning, seek the favours of women with every kind of lewd-ness.[43]

This account should not be taken too literally. William enjoyed poor relations with the church, and this coloured the opinions of clerics and monks about him and his lifestyle.[44] Orderic, moreover, wrote with the benefit of hindsight, and, in this description had a didactic purpose: he contrasted the behaviour of William and his courtiers with the better conduct of their predecessors. We are, here, in the familiar territory of the 'good old days'. Also, William was a bachelor: the absence from his household of a queen may perhaps have contributed to the behaviour of the court. On many occasions, moreover, the atmosphere in William's court was military in tone. It was also a young court: many of his immediate entourage were married, but there were also a fair proportion of bachelors. Lively, it very probably was, but it would be a mistake to assume it was necessarily a hotbed of vice, or an overly dangerous environment for a young woman. The absence of a queen did not mean the total absence of respectable women: the wives, mothers and sisters of courtiers will have been present on formal occasions. Nest, if she came to William's court, would have probably had chaperones. As a royal ward, some-one would have been appointed to have charge of her.

When might Nest have met Henry, if, indeed, they did meet at this stage of her life? To answer this, it is necessary to look at Henry's life as a young man, and to examine the evidence regarding his movements. He was older than Nest by some years, being born most probably in 1068.[45] He was the youngest of the sons of William the Conqueror and his wife Matilda, and the only one to be born in England, where he was probably also educated. He cannot, as a child, have anticipated becoming king: he possessed three older brothers.[46] He had been knighted by his father in May 1086, and subsequently accompanied William the Conqueror back to Normandy, being present at Saint-Gervais, near Rouen with his father when the latter died in September of 1087. William left Normandy to his eldest son Robert, and England to William Rufus: Henry received only a large sum of money, and, perhaps, the hope of inheriting lands left by his mother in England.[47] It cannot have been a comfortable position. It is difficult, at a distance of nearly a thousand years, to draw conclusions about the kinds of affective bonds which may have existed between the children of William the Conqueror, and we possess no direct evidence as to their feeling for one another. It seems, however, that none of his sons was wholly content with his disposition of his properties, and neither were their various friends and followers. Robert apparently felt disgruntled at not receiving England, and a notable section of the senior nobility – including the Conqueror's half-brother, Odo bishop of Bayeux, supported him. William Rufus had designs on Normandy. Henry, left landless, must have had concerns about establishing himself long-term, which required lands as well as financial resources. To begin with, he remained in Normandy, enjoying good terms with his brother Robert. In 1088, Robert made him count of Western Normandy, in return for a large loan to help fund a planned invasion of England which never, in fact, materialised. Perhaps encouraged by this fraternal generosity, however, Henry travelled to England for the first time since his father's death in July 1088. He was seeking his mother's lands from William Rufus, but the latter refused, and Henry soon returned to Normandy.

He had already begun to form bonds of loyalty with his lords and vassals in western Normandy, and it may be that Robert Curthose felt this to be threatening.[48] In Henry's absence, and with the encouragement of Odo of Bayeux, Robert had decided Henry was a danger and was conspiring against him with William Rufus. On his return, far from being welcomed, Henry found himself deprived of his lands and imprisoned at Bayeux, where he remained until some time in 1089. In 1090, he was back at Robert's court, but any trust there had been between the brothers must have evaporated. Nevertheless he fought alongside Robert against William, who had invaded Normandy, and earned himself the reputation of a hero in battle at Rouen.[49] Perhaps as a reward for this, perhaps through necessity, he became count of western Normandy again by 1091.

His return to favour proved short-lived. William Rufus invaded Normandy for a second time in February 1091. This time, he negotiated a settlement with Robert without coming to battle. Under this, the two elder sons of the Conqueror agreed to partition the duchy between them and made each other their heirs, omitting Henry. The latter lacked the necessary power base to resist his brothers, and, after being besieged by them for a time at Mont-Saint-Michel, he surrendered and left Normandy for France, remaining in exile there for around a year.[50] His exile might have been longer, were it not that, in December 1091, Robert and William quarrelled. This provided a new opportunity to the young Henry, who seems to have begun once again to build for himself a network of friends and allies. He soon acquired himself a new holding – the key fortress of Domfront in south-west Normandy, which he apparently gained through the connivance of its castellan.[51] From here, he rebuilt his power in western Normandy, although he probably also earned himself the enmity of Robert de Bellême, to whom Domfront had belonged. He also forged a new, amicable, relationship with William Rufus, which was to endure until the latter's death in 1100. It appears, from what we know of him, that Henry was an intelligent man: William had already had one serious illness. Kings and dukes at this period were expected not only to plan military campaigns but to participate in the fighting. Henry may well already have been weighing his chances of inheriting from one brother or the other. Robert had been the more generous with him, but had also proved the more unreliable. Additionally, Robert's rule in Normandy had proved troubled: in 1094, his arrangement with William Rufus had been abandoned, and he had financial difficulties. Henry may well have concluded that William Rufus was a better potential friend and ally. In 1094, William returned to Normandy and asked Henry to aid him against Robert: Henry agreed, and travelled to England on his brother's invitation.[52] The two met on 29 December, and Henry remained with his brother for several months.

This provides us with the first point at which Henry might have met Nest. Her father had been killed in spring 1093, and she had probably been captured some time in the next few months. William Rufus did not come to Wales until the autumn of 1095, but this does not rule out the possibility that he may already have required Arnulf or Earl Hugh to surrender Nest to him. One might, perhaps, picture her at William's Christmas court in late 1094, in the charge of a trusted guardian, perhaps only speaking limited French and not completely understanding all that went on around her. Certainly, she is unlikely at this point in time to have understood the complicated politics binding England and Normandy. Henry in 1094 was twenty-five or twenty-six, Nest perhaps thirteen or fourteen. This seems very young to modern eyes, but in the late eleventh century, this was old enough to marry and to bear children. There is nothing about this date to distinguish it from the other occasions on which Nest may have met Henry: if anything, it is probably too early. We are in the land of supposition and guesswork, but it seems to me unlikely that Nest came into the sphere of William Rufus – if, indeed, she ever did – as early as the winter of 1095/6. At this time, she was probably still in the hands of her captor or some chosen guardian family.

In September 1096, Robert Curthose came to a new agreement with William Rufus. The Pope, Urban II, had called for what became the First Crusade in February of the same year, and Robert had determined to go. He required money, however: thus, he pawned

Normandy to William Rufus for ten thousand silver marks and set off.[53] What of Henry? Robert of Torigny tells us that he henceforth remained with William wherever the latter went.[54] Certainly, he accompanied his brother on campaign in the Vexin in 1097–8, and we know he was in England in May 1099 and in August 1100. He must have spent at least some time on his estates in Normandy (which William had confirmed to him), but these visits could well have coincided with William's trips to Normandy. These took place from September 1096 to April 1097; November 1097 to April 1099; and June 1099 to early autumn 1099. So, if Robert of Torigny was correct, Henry was in England with his brother in the spring and summer of 1097, part of spring 1099, and from the autumn of 1099 onwards.[55]

Did Henry accompany William on the latter's Welsh campaign in the spring of 1097? We do not know. It is tempting to think so, for this provides one possible context in which he may have encountered not only Nest, but also Sybil Corbet, perhaps at the court of Earl Hugh of Shrewsbury, or of his neighbour, Earl Hugh of Chester.

In the spring of 1097, Henry would have been approaching his thirtieth birthday: a seasoned warrior and politician, and also an experienced lover of women. He was to have at least twenty illegitimate children, more than any other English king, and most of these were probably conceived in the years before his coronation and marriage in 1100. As the son of one king and the brother of another, he may have cut an appealing figure in the eyes of young women. His tumultuous career after the death of William the Conqueror probably also lent him an air of excitement. Yet we should not be too romantic in our view of him, as this was a pragmatic age, and young women who knew they had little or no chance of marrying a prince or a high-born nobleman would nevertheless have been quick to realise the potential advantages to themselves and their families of becoming the mistress of such a man. As we will see, moreover, having been Henry's mistress was not necessarily a bar when it came to achieving a respectable marriage subsequently.

The chronicler William of Malmesbury, a later contemporary of Henry, has left us a description of him:

In person, he was less than short and less than tall, with black hair retreating from his forehead, a glance serene and kindly, muscular chest and thick set limbs. In season, he was full of fun and once he had decided to be sociable, a mass of business did not damp his spirits.[56]

It is hard to judge, at this distance, how such a man might have struck a girl in her mid-teens. Nest, in 1097, will have been aged about fifteen, give or take a year or two. By both the customs of her Welsh heritage, and those of her Norman captors, she was quite old enough to be married — or seduced. Her value and status were probably the subject of some concern. As she matured, the potential danger she represented increased, and if she married the wrong man, her ancestry might be exploited in ways that were highly undesirable, from the point of view of William Rufus. Perhaps she was attracting attention from land-hungry lords from the Welsh borders. By 1097, Arnulf de Bellême may have given up any plans he might have had to marry her himself, but there were plenty of other lords of lower rank with lands or claims in or near Wales, and ambitions to expand. William Rufus was probably in no hurry to see her married. He must also have known of her two brothers, and realised that the exiled Gruffudd ap Rhys ap Tewdwr would be growing up. It may be that by the later 1090s, William or his advisers were contemplating a suitable marriage for her, or perhaps a convent. Henry was almost certainly not part of William's plans. But, as has been mentioned, he was an enthusiastic pursuer of women.

Nest has left the reputation of having been beautiful. What did this mean to her contemporaries? Standards of beauty vary from time to time and place to place, and no physical description of her has survived. Her grandson Gerald, who may not have known her in person, tells us only that she was high-born and noble, a fact from which he derived considerable pride.[57] The Welsh prose tales set considerable store by high birth and gracious behaviour in their descriptions of beautiful female characters. We are told of Arawn's wife in *Pwyll* that she was 'the most beautiful woman anyone had seen',[58] but the nature of this beauty is not described – we learn, rather, that she was dressed in gold brocade and that she was 'gracious in disposition and conversation'.[59] In the same tale, when Pwyll encounters Rhiannon, 'it seemed to him that the beauty of every girl and woman he had seen was nothing compared to this face of this lady'.[60] But again, the emphasis is placed not on her face or figure, but on her generosity and charm – and her intelligence, which she uses to benefit her lover. Branwen is 'the most beautiful girl in the world',[61] but again, no details are given. We are given a more detailed account of Olwen:

> Her hair was yellower than broom, her skin whiter than sea-foam, her palms and fingers were whiter than shoots of marsh trefoil against the sand of a welling spring. Neither the eye of a mewed hawk nor the eye of a thrice mewed falcon was fairer than hers: her breasts were whiter than the breast of a white swan; her cheeks were redder than the reddest foxgloves …[62]

The image is interesting for a number of reasons. The references to flora that would be recognisable to a Welsh audience locates it within that culture. But it also reflects the value placed on rank and status: Olwen's skin is white. This is a girl who does not need to undertake any form of outside labour: she can afford to protect her skin from sun or wind, because of the wealth of her father. Her hands, too, are white: she does not undertake manual work. Her red cheeks suggest health; her yellow hair perhaps reflects an additional value placed on rarity – but we have no way of knowing how common blond or red hair was in Wales at this time.

Is this a distinctively Welsh idea of beauty? The question of the relationship of the Welsh prose tales to French, English and other compositions is complex, and I do not propose to address it here. However, it is perhaps worth noting in passing that in the *Lais* attributed to Marie de France and composed in the later twelfth century we find this description of another heroine:

> Her body was comely, her hips low, her neck whiter than snow on a branch; her eyes were bright and her face white, her mouth fair and her

nose well-placed; her eyebrows were brown and her brow fair, and her hair curly and rather blond. A gold thread does not shine as brightly as the rays reflected in the light from her hair.[63]

The author of the *Lais* speaks of Breton sources or influences upon them, but I would hesitate before assuming that this lends any specific 'Celtic' context to the descriptions. I have argued above that it is inappropriate to compare Welsh materials with those from Ireland, Brittany or any other of the 'Celtic' regions. What we have in the extract given above is less likely to reflect 'Celticity' than the effects of the common Anglo-Norman context in which these stories were recorded. We meet golden hair and fair skin also in the romances of Chrétien de Troyes, another late twelfth-century writer.[64]

As far as Nest is concerned, her education and upbringing would probably have taught her how to converse charmingly and how to please; also, she could have been protected from manual labour, giving her the desirable signs of wealth – soft hands and untanned skin. As to whether she was dark or fair, we cannot know. Gerald of Wales has left us a brief description of her son Maurice – a man of medium height and high complexion, possessed of good manners.[65] Raymond, her grandson, is also described 'a little taller than average, with flaxen, slightly curly hair, great round, grey eyes, a rather prominent nose, a high complexion, and a cheerful and composed expression.'[66] Raymond was the son of Nest's eldest son William. Did he derive his fair hair from his grandmother? We do not know. We can only say that she possessed some quality, be it in appearance, or charm, or intelligence, which was to attract to her a series of men of rank and position.

She was certainly not Henry's first mistress. As has been mentioned, by 1097, he was an experienced lover of women, and already had a number of illegitimate children. His first known mistress seems to have been the mother of his eldest son, Robert, who would later on become Earl of Gloucester. As Crouch has shown, this woman was a member of the Gay family of Oxfordshire.[67] This family was respectable, but not of the upper aristocracy, and for a daughter to become the mistress of a king's son was more an advantage than a source of shame. The elevation of this lady's son to the high nobility was to raise his maternal kinsfolk, also.[68] Henry may have met her in around 1084, and Robert seems to have been born around 1090.[69] In this instance, at least, Henry seems to have formed a relationship which lasted some years, and he was greatly attached to Robert. Robert's mother is obscure: we know rather more about other mistresses, and their histories help throw some light upon Nest and her relation to the king.

Robert's mother was probably single, but this was not always the case with Henry's mistresses. His next oldest known child, Richard, was born to him by a married woman, one Ansfrida. It seems that through her relationship with Henry, she was able to protect the interests of her other, legitimate son, even though his father, her husband, had been imprisoned by William Rufus.[70] In the case of a third mistress, Edith daughter of Forn, Henry arranged a marriage for her.[71]

Sybil Corbet, whom Nest may perhaps have known – or even grown up with – became the mother of Henry's son Rainald, who would later rise to be Earl of Cornwall and died in 1175.[72] Sybil was an heiress: she had no brothers, and, as a result, the lands of her father Robert Corbet were divided between her and her sister. There was probably no question, however, of her managing her inheritance alone, and, like Edith, she too married after her relationship with Henry. Her husband was Herbert fitz Herbert, and their descendants established themselves as a baronial house.[73] It is possible that Sybil may have borne Henry more than one child: like the mother of Robert, she may have had a liaison of several years with him.[74]

Did Henry make Sybil his mistress on his visit to England in 1094/5? This must be a possibility – although, as with so much to do with Nest, we cannot know for sure. But it could be that it was to Sybil that Nest owed her first introduction to Henry. Perhaps in 1097 Sybil contacted her lover – and drew his attention, perhaps accidentally, to her former foster-sister. The two young women might have met each other again at court, and Sybil might have then presented Nest to Henry. This is, it must be stressed, speculation: one must also allow for the possibility that the two women were never acquainted. But, as has been suggested, some connexion may have existed.

Sybil was probably a little older than Nest, but as has been said, she may have enjoyed a liaison of several years with Henry. It is unclear how long Nest held his attention. Henry was very probably not faithful to any one of his mistresses. They do not, as far as we know, seem to have travelled with him, and he very probably enjoyed a number of simultaneous relationships with women in different places in England and Normandy. The number of children a given woman had with him may reflect as much on how frequently they met as on how long they were involved: a mistress based in one of his regular haunts would be likely to receive more attention than one he saw rarely due to distance. A young woman in Nest's position would not have been able to travel easily: she had no resources of her own, and she would not have been permitted to wander alone or in any company other than that approved or provided by her guardian or keeper. Her liaison with Henry was probably limited by geography as well as time. The daughters of the lower aristocracy or gentry could seek advancement for themselves or their kin through an affair with Henry, and seem to have had no difficulty in marrying subsequently. Nest, however, was a different case. Her social position must have been debatable, at best. William Rufus was unlikely to allow her to be regarded as heiress to all Deheubarth, however much an ambitious suitor might wish for that. Yet without that claim, she had little or no value: she had no land or property of her own, and, as such, there was little or no incentive for anyone to marry her. It may well be that the king – and Nest's guardian, whoever that was – saw a convent as the safest destination for her.

By becoming the mistress of the brother of the king, Nest may have been seeking for an escape from a difficult situation. If we may believe William of Malmesbury, Henry was pleasant and charming, when he wished, and he certainly possessed considerable power and influence. While the initiative for the seduction probably came from

Henry, Nest may well have welcomed his attentions. Other women had gained status or advantage through such a relationship. Nest was probably still in her teens, but this does necessarily mean she would not have had pragmatic aims. This was not a particularly romantic period of history. Having Henry's child would give her a certain position – Henry seems to have been good about providing for his illegitimate children and, therefore, for their mothers. It would, however, have made her far less likely to find herself confined to a convent. She may also have seen Henry as a powerful potential protector against the likes of Arnulf of Montgomery. We do not know what she thought about the new Norman lords of south Wales, but she may well have disliked, resented or even hated the man who had colonised her father's lands. Arnulf's character remains shadowy in our extant sources, but his elder brother Robert de Bellême left the reputation of a cruel and cold man. If Arnulf resembled him, it is unsurprising if Nest shrank from the idea of finding herself married to him. Henry was powerful enough to protect her against such marriage, and he had considerable influence with William Rufus, who was probably the arbiter of her fate in these years. Whatever the ins and outs of the situation, it could well be in the last years of the eleventh century that Nest became the mistress of Henry, and bore him a son, also named Henry.

As has been seen with Edith daughter of Forn and Sybil Corbet, having an illegitimate child with a royal father was not necessarily a problem for a woman at this time. Attitudes to illegitimacy were still flexible, at least amongst the upper echelons, and even the clergy could and did make excuses. William of Malmesbury added a brief explanation to his description of Henry of the latter's pre- and extra-marital liaisons as motivated not through lust but through a desire to beget children.[75] Henry, it must be said, seems to have been attached to his children, legitimate and well as illegitimate. But, as Eleanor Searle has pointed out, this may have been rooted in more than just affection.[76]

It has been seen, both in the case of Wales and in the problems experienced by William Rufus, Robert Curthose and Henry in

Normandy and England in the 1080s and 1090s that a strong and reliable base of loyal supporters was of great importance to a king or a lord in his maintenance of power. After victory at the battle of Mynydd Carn, Gruffudd ap Cynan was unable to impose himself over Gwynedd, as he lacked support from the *uchelwyr*. Unable to be certain of the loyalty of Roger of Montgomery and other powerful Marcher lords, William opened up Wales to them, as both a source of land and as a diversion for their warlike tendencies. Henry had learnt to his cost in western Normandy that without the backing of the local nobility, he could not retain his lands and power there. It has been demonstrated by Searle, Newman and Hollister how, as king, Henry was able to make use of his illegitimate children to strengthen existing bonds with the nobility and royalty of neighbouring lands, to enhance existing bonds and to reinforce his power in debatable territories.[77] William, who pre-deceased him, and Matilda. He gave the latter in marriage at the age of eight to the Holy Roman Emperor, a valuable ally. His illegitimate daughters might not look so high, but the majority of them married far better than their mothers' backgrounds might have indicated. Sybil, perhaps a daughter of Sybil Corbet, married Alexander I, king of Scotland and brother to Henry's wife Edith-Matilda.[78] Maud married Count Rotrou of Perche, a key ally in Normandy of Henry, especially against the troublesome Robert de Bellême.[79] Another daughter, also named Maud, married the count of Brittany.[80] This strategy was not restricted to Henry I: his grandson, Henry II, gave an illegitimate daughter, Emma, to Dafydd ap Owain of Gwynedd, and, perhaps most famously, King John married his illegitimate daughter Joanna to Llywelyn the Great. At least in the eleventh, twelfth and early thirteenth centuries, the illegitimate daughter of the king of England was considered a perfectly suitable and appropriate bride for one of his major vassals or even a neighbouring ruler of lesser stature.

Illegitimate daughters provided a king with a useful way to buy or consolidate alliances, but illegitimate sons could be rather more problematic. In Wales, the distinction between legitimate and illegitimate sons was to remain blurred down into the thirteenth century.

Llywelyn the Great seems to have wished to leave Gwynedd to his younger, legitimate son Dafydd (perhaps not least because the latter was the grandson of King John and nephew of Henry III), but at least some of his nobility preferred his elder son Gruffudd, despite the latter's illegitimacy, and Gruffudd himself felt his claim to be as good or better than Dafydd's.[81] It remained common throughout the twelfth centuries for Welsh rulers to have children with several different women, and for all their sons – save any born to slaves – to feel entitled to make an attempt at winning rulership for themselves. From Nest's point of view, having an illegitimate child may well not have seemed to be a major issue. The Norman situation was a little more difficult: certainly, William the Conqueror had succeeded to the duchy of Normandy despite being illegitimate, but he had faced considerable resistance on account of this.[82] His kingship of England rested largely on right of conquest. By the beginning of the twelfth century, it is unlikely that an illegitimate heir might have succeeded to power in England or Normandy. When, in November 1120, Henry I's legitimate son was drowned in the wreck of the White Ship, he did not – and probably could not – propose any of his illegitimate sons as the new heir. Male royal bastards were perhaps less welcome than female ones: they had to be provided for and they might create problems. On the other hand, they would owe any rank and status they achieved to their father, and as such might be expected to be loyal. This, certainly, was the experience of Henry I with his illegitimate sons. It should, however, be noted that in general, the provision made for them was no more than respectable.[83] Henry only raised up one of his illegitimate sons to the high nobility. This was Robert of Gloucester, who was perhaps a special case. He seems to have been the eldest of Henry's children, and, more to the point, he was loyal and devoted, not only Henry himself, but, as it transpired, to his legitimate half-sister Matilda, whom Henry made his heir on the death of William. Henry may have avoided elevating his other illegitimate sons to avoid incurring the anger or jealousy of the aristocracy. He was not alone in having illegitimate children, however: his brother Robert Curthose seems to have had at least two.[84] Two illegitimate sons of Earl Hugh of Chester served under Henry I, one as abbot of Bury St Edmunds, the other as a royal messenger and tutor.[85] This was not yet a period or a culture in which bastardy was automatically a stigma or a bar to office. When Nest gave birth to Henry's son, she could probably be sure that Henry would provide for both of them. Henry must have been notified of the arrival of this son, although we cannot know how he reacted. William Rufus, however, may have been pleased. While the men of the lower nobility and gentry would accept the former mistresses of a king or prince as bride, the proud and ambitious Arnulf of Montgomery almost certainly would not. One of the dangers presented by the existence of a daughter of the last king of Deheubarth had been neutralised.

4

NEST AND THE REBELS

In the medieval period, the death of a king carried with it considerable side effects. We have seen how the killing of Rhys ap Tewdwr in 1093 caused immense upheaval for his daughter. On 2 August 1100, William Rufus, accompanied by his younger brother Henry and a number of his leading courtiers, set out to hunt in the New Forest, where he met his death in a hunting accident. He had never married and he left no son as heir. Henry set out at once for the royal court of Winchester. William Rufus had abandoned his former agreement with Robert Curthose, which would have made the latter his heir, but Henry did not wish to take chances.[1] Three days later, on 5 August, he was crowned at Westminster. The haste was necessary: Robert Curthose had not abandoned his claim to the English throne, and he still had powerful supporters amongst the nobility, not least the troublesome Robert de Bellême and his brother, Arnulf of Montgomery, lord of Pembroke.

Robert de Bellême had inherited the Norman lands of his father, Roger of Montgomery, while his second brother Hugh became Earl of Shrewsbury. Hugh, however, had been killed in 1098 by the king of Norway, while besieging Cadwgan ab Bleddyn and Gruffudd ap Cynan on Anglesey. Robert had succeeded to his brother's English lands and titles. As Earl of Shrewsbury, he was now a major magnate in England as well as Normandy, and, as we have seen before, he was no friend to the new Henry I, who had deprived him of Domfront in Normandy. Robert and his brother had supported Robert Curthose against William Rufus in the rebellion of 1088: Henry was almost certainly anticipating trouble from that direction. His rapid coronation was designed to legitimise his claim to the throne as fast as possible. Within months, he married, doubtless determined to provide himself with a legitimate heir in the near future. His bride was Edith-Matilda of Scotland, herself a descendant of the old Anglo-Saxon kings of England. Henry was mustering as many ways as possible to bolster his – and his putative heir's – claim to England.[2] To begin with, at least, he seems to have decided to remain faithful to his new wife. If Nest was still his mistress at this point, the affair probably ended. We do not know where she was at the death of William, but, if she had become Henry's mistress by this time and borne his son, it is likely he had ensured she was provided for somewhere, perhaps lodging her with one of his vassals, perhaps settling her in a small household of her own (the former seems more likely). She, as well as Henry, may have been wondering what the Bellême brothers might be about to do: they had already played a large role in her life, and it is not impossible that Arnulf was disgruntled by her seduction by another man.

At the end of the eleventh century, Robert de Bellême was one of the richest and most powerful men anywhere in the Norman territories. In Normandy, he held the lordships of Alençon, Montgommery, Bellême, Argentan and Falaise. To this he had added Pontieu, through marriage to its heiress, Agnes, daughter of Count Guy of Pontieu. Several of these areas were sensitive key holdings along the Norman border with France, with the result that his support was of great importance to whoever was in control of Normandy. In England, along with the earldom of Shrewsbury, he had extensive lands in Sussex and controlled the strategically significant castles at Arundel and Tickhill. Although since the death of William the Conqueror, the Bellême brothers had tended to support Robert Curthose, this support had not been unwavering and it was founded more on self-interest than on genuine loyalty. Robert de Bellême had backed

Duke Robert in 1090 against William Rufus, he had in 1092 made an attempt to secede from Normandy altogether and to become instead a vassal of the king of France, thus threatening the borders of that duchy.[3] His dominant motivation seems to have been self-interest and the maintenance of the power and status of his family: no king or duke could afford to be reliant upon him. In 1098, his acquisition of the earldom of Shrewsbury was to the detriment of his younger brother Arnulf, who seems to have been more closely associated with Earl Hugh and who may have been considered as his heir.[4] Yet Arnulf remained close to him: it seems that he, too, was concerned with family honour and influence.

Orderic Vitalis has left us a description of the character of Robert de Bellême in his *Ecclesiastical History*:

> He was a man of keen intelligence, treacherous and devious, strong and well-built, bold and victorious in battle, ready in speech and appallingly cruel, insatiable in his greed and lust. He was ingenious in devising difficult enterprises and ready to endure unremitting toil in worldly ventures. He showed great skill both in planning buildings and devising siege-weapons and other such things; but he was a merciless butcher in the way he tortured men. He never honoured, aided, or clothed Mother Church as a son should, but like a stepson shamed, oppressed and plundered her … He humbled many by seizing their honours and burning their castles, or reduced them to penury by ravaging their lands, or, still worse, mutilated them, leaving them maimed or halt or blind and utterly helpless.[5]

Orderic was no fan of Earl Robert, who he seems to have regarded as a true son of the infamous Mabel de Bellême. Robert's recorded actions, however, hint that Orderic's assessment may have been based on more than just dislike and exaggeration. He was a man that no king or duke could afford to ignore, and he seems to have revelled in his power.

In August 1100, however, on the coronation of Henry I as the new king of England, Robert set sail for England from Normandy to do homage. We cannot know if he was in any way sincere: given his history, it is likely that he was respecting the conventions, deflecting any chance of immediate hostility from Henry, and gauging the atmosphere at the new court. Was Henry likely to interfere with him or his brother, or to attempt to curtail his power? He may have left feeling reassured that this was unlikely, so in the early months of his reign, Henry found the nobility less than welcoming.[6] In September 1100, Robert Curthose returned from his crusade, and Henry was in no position to attempt to prevent his elder brother from resuming control over Normandy. During the winter of 1101, Robert began to make plans for an invasion of England. Robert de Bellême seems to have been amongst his supporters.

Duke Robert launched his invasion in the summer of 1101, at which time Robert de Bellême was in England. Yet no battle ensued: instead, Duke Robert met with Henry at Alton, in Hampshire and a peace settlement was negotiated between them by a number of leading barons – including Robert de Bellême.

Under the terms of this new agreement, Robert abandoned his claim to England, and Henry surrendered his Normandy holdings, with the exception of Domfront.[7] Robert de Bellême is unlikely to have been pleased at this outcome – the loss of Domfront rankled. But he remained in England, observing and perhaps determining whether or not he would, in the long run, be able to manipulate Henry to his own advantage.

It seems he decided that he could not. He had enemies at Henry's court, notably Robert, count of Meulan, who was one of Henry's foremost advisors and a long-lasting enemy of Robert de Bellême.[8] He began to lay plans against Henry, preferring the weaker Robert Curthose as an overlord. He was aware, also, that Henry distrusted him: he had supported Robert in 1101 and begun constructing a powerful castle at Bridgenorth without royal permission. He must have anticipated that punishment of some kind would eventually be forthcoming.

It soon materialised: Robert de Bellême and his brother Arnulf were summoned to Winchester in the spring of 1102 and accused of a long string of offences.[9] They had made their preparations:

...they occupied their castles and fortified them, and summoned help to
them from all sides and summoned to them the Britons who were under
them, together with their leaders, namely the sons of Bleddyn ap Cynfyn,
Cadwgan, Iorwerth and Maredudd.[10]

We have met Cadwgan ab Bleddyn before: he was Nest's second
cousin. He had twice invaded Deheubarth during her childhood,[11]
and during the 1090s become the prime mover and focus of the
Welsh rebellion against the Norman invaders of Wales. Whether
Nest had met him by this stage we do not know, but he must have
been well known to the Bellême brothers, and especially to Arnulf,
as a determined enemy. Robert may have considered himself to be
Cadwgan's feudal overlord: the earldom of Montgomery bordered
on Powys and had probably made inroads into parts of Powysian
territory. Nelson has suggested that one of Robert's first acts as the
new Earl of Shrewsbury had been to draw up an agreement of some
kind with Cadwgan in 1099, under which the latter received parts
of Powys and Ceredigion, in return for becoming Robert's vassal.[12] Cadwgan's attitude to Robert is harder to establish. It is highly
unlikely that he accepted Robert's feudal definition of their relationship, yet at the same time he will have been keenly aware of the
danger Robert could present to him. It appears that he had defied
Robert's brother and predecessor Earl Hugh. He will, moreover,
have noted that Robert's time and attention was divided between
England and Normandy, and he may have hoped to exploit this.
Robert de Bellême was nothing if not practical, and he will have
observed the problems created in Wales and the March by Cadwgan
and his associates in the 1090s. He recognised a useful, resourceful
neighbour who could become either a valuable ally or an enemy,
and who was connected by blood or alliance to most of the leading
men of Wales. In 1099, it was in the interests of both men to come
to terms, but we should not imagine that either expected their alliance to endure. The years between 1099 and 1102 were peaceful for
Cadwgan, allowing him to rebuild his network of connexions and
to co-ordinate with his two younger brothers. The death in 1101

of Earl Hugh of Shrewsbury and the accession of his heir, who was only seven years old, had relieved pressure on his northern borders. In 1102, Cadwgan was looking to expand. An alliance – which he may well have expected to be temporary – with his Bellême neighbours provided him with an opportunity to do this – and with a highly effective and powerful military buffer zone against the king of England. In 1102, Robert, Arnulf and Cadwgan all shared a common goal: a disruption of the power of Henry and his supporters and a desire to benefit from the consequences of this.

Robert de Bellême did not restrict his search for allies to Wales, however. Arnulf was still unmarried, and he may not have abandoned the idea of finding a bride with links to a non-Norman royal family. Nest was no longer an option, but he had another neighbour: Muirchertach ua Briain, the most powerful king in Ireland. He sent Gerald of Windsor to Muirchertach, requesting a marriage alliance.[13] The request was granted, and along with his new wife, Arnulf secured military backing from Muirchertach. This new relationship opened yet another in its wake, for through it, Arnulf became a brother-in-law of the king of Norway, who was to marry another of Muirchertach's daughters. Robert de Bellême sought an alliance with Magnus, also. Perhaps fortunately for Henry I, Magnus refused.

Even without a Norwegian ally, Robert was at first in a strong position, and he and Arnulf prepared themselves for civil war. Their castles throughout England – from Arundel in Sussex to Tickhill in Yorkshire – were placed on a war footing, their allies, including Cadwgan, were summoned, and additionally they hired mercenaries.[14]

Henry mustered a considerable force against them: it seems he was determined to put an end to his troubles with Robert de Bellême once and for all. The Bellême strongholds of Lincoln and Arundel were besieged. He also decided to try and break up the power-bloc possessed by Robert and Arnulf. He summoned Iorwerth ab Bleddyn, Cadwgan's younger brother, to him and offered him not only Cadwgan's lands in Powys and Ceredigion but also lands in Dyfed, Cydweli, Gower and Ystrad Tywi, in return for Iorwerth's support.

Iorwerth ab Bleddyn is an interesting figure. He was certainly younger than Cadwgan — perhaps the youngest of the sons of Bleddyn — and if he had been old enough to be involved in any of Cadwgan's activities in the 1090s, it has not been recorded. It is clear that he harboured ambitions of his own, and it may be that he felt excluded or overshadowed by his elder brother. It seems, too, that Cadwgan may have been closer to his other surviving brother, Maredudd, than to Iorwerth.[15] Iorwerth may have been concerned that he would lose out to his brothers over time. He may had held some personal enmity towards Robert or Arnulf or both.[16] He may have been impressed by Henry: we cannot know exactly what his motivations were. But, having met with Henry or his representatives, he turned on his brothers and the Bellême brothers, and ravaged Robert's lands in Shropshire and the March.

The tide was turning against Robert: first Arundel and then Tickhill castles fell to Henry's forces, while his own expeditions, aided by the forces of Cadwgan and Maredudd, sons of Bleddyn, met with less success. By the autumn of 1102, Bridgenorth castle had also fallen, and Robert was in retreat. Henry advanced on Shrewsbury, the last major stronghold in England left to Robert. At this point, Robert seems to have accepted the inevitable; he 'went out to meet the king as he approached the town, confessed his treachery, and handed over the keys of the whole town to the conqueror.'[17] It was the end of Robert de Bellême's power in England: deprived of the earldom of Shropshire and all his other lands in the country, he returned to Normandy, where he carried over his resentment at his treatment into a campaign against Robert Curthose. The latter had incurred his anger by supporting Henry during the rebellion and attacking Robert de Bellême's castle of Vignats. Robert de Bellême did not forgive or forget. When Henry I gained control of Normandy in 1106, Robert de Bellême continued to be a thorn in his side. Finally, on 4 November 1112, Henry arrested and imprisoned him for the rest of his life.

What of Arnulf?[18] When Robert surrendered in 1102, Arnulf was not present, but it seems that Henry sent messengers to him granting him permission to hand over all his English and Welsh lands and to leave for Normandy. The alternative was to submit formally to Henry: Arnulf chose exile and went into Normandy to his brother Robert. He was now effectively landless, and Robert took no steps to remedy this. At this point the previous amity between the brothers broke, and Arnulf joined Robert Curthose's campaign against his brother. His dominant ambition was now the acquisition of a new lordship: in 1103, we find him once again in Ireland, where he seems to have hopes of aid from his Irish father-in-law, Muirchertach. But he had lost his usefulness. According to Orderic Vitalis, far from offering him lands or support, Muirchertach reclaimed his daughter and drove Arnulf out.[19] Thereafter it seems he remained mainly in Normandy, perhaps dependent on the dubious goodwill of his elder brother.

What does this rebellion have to do with Nest? We do not know where she was during it, or what she was doing. It should be pointed out that autumn 1102, when Henry came to Shropshire, provides us with another window during which she may have met the king and become, however briefly, his mistress. This, however, is unlikely for another reason, as will be shown. Henry's victory over the Montgomery family, and his acquisition of their lands, were to bring Nest back not only to Wales, but to Dyfed, the land of her childhood.

Arnulf de Bellême had not spent his entire time in his earldom of Pembrokeshire, and, by 1102, he had introduced reliable men whose task was not only to administer and control his lands, but to defend them against the Welsh and to push back their borders. Key amongst these men was his constable, Gerald of Windsor, whom we have met before. Gerald held Pembroke Castle for Arnulf and was his senior representative in Wales. By 1102, he was a seasoned warrior, well-accustomed to his duties. He possessed invaluable experience in dealing with the Welsh, both in war and in peace: he knew the terrain, he knew the leading men. Although of a minor family and although he probably held little or no land of his own, he was a significant man, at least within south-west Wales, and, from the point of view of Henry I, he was useful. Henry had little or no direct experience of Wales in 1102, but he knew he had to make arrangements to secure the lands he had taken from Robert and Arnulf. He needed someone effective upon whom he might rely. He was eventually to choose Gerald of Windsor.

At first it seems a strange choice: Gerald was Arnulf's man, after all. The little that we know of him between the invasion of Deheubarth in 1093 and 1102 shows this. In 1097, he had attacked the lands of the church of St Davids, whose bishop had shown himself no friend to the Norman invaders.[20] As Arnulf's representative, it was for Gerald to discourage activities against his overlord and to reduce or remove the resources of his enemies, even if within the church. His grandson Gerald of Wales, who seems not to have known him personally, has not left us a physical description, but did speak of his grandfather's stalwartness and intelligence.[21] During Robert and Arnulf's rebellion, Gerald remained loyal to his overlord: indeed, it was to him that Arnulf entrusted the sensitive task of travelling to Ireland and negotiating with Muirchertach ua Briain. We do not know where he was when Arnulf received Henry's message offering him the choice of absolute submission or exile, but it is probable that he was at Pembroke Castle. It appears that at this point, he did not accompany his lord into exile. Perhaps he was unable to do so. Perhaps the news of Arnulf's flight only reached him after the event. Perhaps he simply chose not to.

This would not necessarily have been a dangerous move: the removal of an overlord at this period did not necessarily lead to the dismissal or removal of their vassals, so long as the latter were willing to accept and be loyal to their new lord. It appears that shortly after Arnulf's fall, Gerald met with Henry or with Henry's representatives, and as a result was allowed to remain in south-west Wales in some capacity. Initially, however, he was not allowed to remain at Pembroke: the latter would provide too useful and too defensible an access point into Wales for Arnulf, should Gerald decide to return to his original loyalty. A knight named Saer was given the guardianship of Pembroke.

For Gerald to change his allegiance in this way was not an automatic indication of either weakness or of disloyalty: rather, it reflects the pragmatic attitude necessary for a man of his background. He belonged to what has been defined as a 'service family'.[22] That is to say, he and his kin had gained their rank and status through service to the king, rather than by accident of birth. His father had served as a steward under William I. William had more than one steward, but it is thought that Gerald's father was probably Walter fitz Other, who held the lordship of Eton and was royal keeper of the forest of Berkshire.[23] If this was indeed the case, then Gerald had brothers who followed their father into service to the king, the church or the greater nobility: William fitz Walter was keeper of the forest of Windsor and subsequently Constable of that castle; Maurice fitz Walter became steward of the abbey of Bury St Edmunds.[24] Before the Norman Conquest, we know nothing of any member of this line, although clearly they had not been significant land-holders in Normandy. Walter was most probably the younger son of a minor lord who followed either Duke William or one of his larger vassals into England and established himself there. Families such as these lacked lands or resources to fall back on: they needed royal or high aristocratic favour in order to survive and to maintain their position. For Gerald, the exile of Arnulf de Bellême could have been a disaster. He had little or nothing to gain by following Arnulf into Normandy: Arnulf held no lands there, and thus had little to offer to a man in Gerald's situation. Robert de Bellême already possessed followers and officers in Normandy, and there was no guarantee that he would make space for Arnulf. In Wales, however, Gerald had his own contacts and probably some land. By remaining, he could hope to retain this. By coming to terms with Henry I he hoped to safeguard what he had already gained, and to put himself in a position to advance to further status via service to this new overlord. Essentially, Gerald seems to have decided that his loyalties should lie with the earldom of Pembroke and whoever was its master, rather than with any one specific individual. He set out to show that he might be useful to Henry, and within a very few years, this policy paid dividends.

Henry made provision for the other parts of Wales which were now in his hands or in his sphere of influence. At first, Gower, Cydweli and Ystrad Tywi came into the hands of Hywel ap Goronwy, who came from the nobility of Buellt. Hywel's father Goronwy had been amongst the allies of Cadwgan ab Bleddyn during the Welsh rebellions of the later 1090s. How much control did Henry have over him? The Welsh Chronicles claim that he owed his new lands to the king, but it may be that Henry chose to ratify a *fait accompli*. It is also possible that Hywel was an associate of Iorwerth ab Bleddyn who had made himself useful to the king in some way – more useful than Iorwerth himself. Hywel was to prove himself to be of debatable value to the king, however, and by 1105 he seems no longer to have enjoyed royal confidence. He was expelled and retaliated by ravaging Ystrad and Rhyd-y-Gors.

Henry apparently did not trust Iorwerth ab Bleddyn: perhaps he had proved of little effective use as an ally against Earl Robert, or perhaps after the end of the rebellion he showed himself disloyal. In 1104, Henry lured him to Shrewsbury and imprisoned him. It is unclear to what extent Iorwerth had gained control over Powys: it is unlikely that in 1102 Henry was in a position to expel Cadwgan ab Bleddyn completely, although he may have raised questions in the minds of the nobility as to the latter's security or legitimacy as its lord. In 1102, Iorwerth had laid hands on his other brother, Maredudd, and sent him to a royal prison – we do not know which one, but Shrewsbury is perhaps the most likely. Cadwgan, however, remained free and active throughout, and it is possible that Hywel ab Goronwy was one of his men, not Iorwerth's – or that Hywel may rapidly have gone over to him, leading to his expulsion in 1105.

As far as Gerald was concerned, he seems to have had a quiet couple of years, in which he was perhaps building his own castle of Carew, as will be discussed below. It seems, however, that he soon proved his loyalty and usefulness to the king: in 1105, Henry confirmed in his role as keeper of Pembroke castle. It proved to be a valuable decision for both parties. Gerald was to serve Henry as loyally and effectively as he had served Arnulf, and he was to be rewarded by enhancement of his status and with the right to hold his own lands, conquered from the Welsh.

It is likely, too, that at this point, Henry remembered Nest. Her connections to the old royal house of Deheubarth were still of significance and she was still unmarried. A lord of the status of Arnulf, as I have argued earlier, would have made an unsuitable husband, being too likely to attempt to exploit her heredity to his own ends. Also, she had been a royal mistress: a member of the high nobility would probably find that unacceptable. She could not be allowed to marry a Welsh lord: that could lend too much influence to rebellion within Wales. Yet at the same time she remained an asset, for it was possible – at least in Norman eyes – that marriage to her might lend to a Norman lord some aura of legitimacy in the eyes of the Welsh populace. At the very least, a Welsh wife might help to reassure the Welsh population that they had a voice of some kind close to the centre of power. Henry tended to provide for his ex-mistresses and their children by him. Arranging a suitable marriage was one way of doing this. It seems very likely that sometime between the autumn of 1102 and 1105, Gerald of Windsor was offered Nest as wife, and accepted. It was a confirmation to him of royal trust, but at the same time it served as a reminder of his rank. As a recent rebel, he was in no position to object to a woman who had been the king's mistress, and he will certainly have recognised her usefulness to him. Henry seems to have considered that Gerald was unlikely to use her family status to his own advantage – probably Gerald knew better, perhaps on account of Welsh law and custom, but more likely on account of his recognition of Henry's ability.[25]

Was Nest consulted over the marriage? If so, it was probably no more than a formality: where political advantage was concerned, the opinions of the woman were of minor significance. She must have had mixed feelings, however. Gerald had been part of the force that invaded and overran her homeland, and he may have been amongst those who captured her and her younger brother Hywel. It is quite likely she had met him in or around 1093. But we do not know what she thought about him, nor how he had treated her as a captive. He did, however, offer her stability and a return to south-west Wales. Did Gerald speak a little Welsh? After his eight or so years of service in south-west Wales, it is possible he had learnt at least some of the language. Certainly, he will have had translators working for him and he will have had some knowledge of Welsh laws and customs. Security was of far greater importance to women of this period than romantic love, and marriage was the main means of acquiring just that.

By 1102, she was familiar with the Anglo-Norman way of life. Nevertheless, she will probably have noted the changes in her native land. Norman keeps now controlled the landscape, and familiar *uchelwyr* were dead or displaced. Arnulf de Bellême had had the first castle at Pembroke constructed, a structure of wood and turf. It may not have differed greatly in appearance from the *llysoedd* of Rhys ap Tewdwr, but the culture inside it was very different. It was a garrison, a working military fortress designed as a stronghold from which ambitious and aggressive fighting men might expand their power and control. The inhabitants were probably mainly male and almost all military in character. It was Gerald's responsibility, but he may not have felt it to be an appropriate place for his new wife. A local tradition holds that upon his marriage, Gerald began the construction of a new castle, some five miles from Pembroke – Carew Castle.[26] This site must have some genuine connexion with Gerald and his family: his descendents through his eldest son by Nest, William, used the surname Carew. It may well be true, therefore, that the original castle owed its origin to Gerald. If so, no structure which can be attributed to him survives now: the extant castle is mainly of fourteenth-century date. It stands on a good defensive site and within easy reach of the centre of the lordship at Pembroke: it would seem to have been an appropriate and logical place for Gerald to build a home for his new wife. We may hope that she liked it.

We do not know how Nest and Gerald felt about each other: there are no letters or tales surviving to give us any clues, and the Welsh Chronicles cannot be considered as fully reliable on this point – as will be seen, for the first part of the twelfth century, they show a marked preference for the Welsh royal house of Powys, with whom Nest was to have dealings. The marriage was to result in at least four children – William, Maurice, David and Angharad – three of whom were born by 1109. The mix of names is interesting – three Norman, one Welsh. That the boys would be given names reflecting their father's background and culture is unsurprising. They, after all, would inherit from him, be associated with him in the public sphere and transmit his name and property to posterity. But the fact that Nest and Gerald named their daughter Angharad is interesting. Perhaps that she was given a Welsh name suggests that Gerald had some sympathy for his wife's language and culture: it might even be a sign of affection. It would be pleasant to think that Nest and Gerald may have learned to like each other, even though their marriage was a matter of political necessity.

In the years before her marriage, Nest had remained mainly in the private sphere that dominated women's lives, but the de Bellême rebellion, and her marriage in its wake, was to involve her much more closely in the wider world, and, in particular with the turbulent political life of early twelfth-century Wales.

On taking charge at Pembroke, Gerald found himself busy. Hywel ap Goronwy's raids of 1105 must have infringed into the territory over which he had responsibility. Gerald will have been amongst those resisting him and trying to reduce the effect of his plundering. The consequences rumbled on into 1106, by which time at least some parts of the Normans in south-west Wales had decided that Hywel must be removed. The men of the castle of Rhyd-y-Gors succeeded in suborning Gwgan ap Meurig, a close associate of Hywel, and, with his help, they were able to ambush and kill Hywel. Gerald was probably not involved personally in this, but the removal of Hywel can only have been to his advantage, and he probably approved the action – or, at least, its consequences. He will have been aware that, despite the Bellême rebellion and the Welsh complicity therein, the years since 1099 had allowed the remaining Welsh royalty and their followers time to rebuild their resources. In the north, the minority of the new earl of Chester had permitted Gruffudd ap Cynan to begin quietly expanding his control outwards from Anglesey. The imprisonment of Iorwerth and Maredudd, sons of Bleddyn, had left

Cadwgan once again in sole control over Powys and perhaps parts of Ceredigion, and able to re-establish his ties of alliance with the *uchelwyr*.

Cadwgan's eldest son, Owain, was approaching adulthood, and in 1106 made his first impression on Welsh political life. He attacked and killed his cousins, Griffri and Meurig, the sons of Trahaearn ap Caradog. As the sons of a former reigning king of Gwynedd and Powys (Trahaearn ap Caradog), they were potential rulers themselves and thus might present a threat to Cadwgan – or to his intermittent ally, Gruffudd ap Cynan. The Norman invasions did not – and perhaps could not – put an end to these traditional rivalries or to the volatility of Welsh politics. Indeed, by their very presence, the Norman lords within Wales became a part of that polity, whether they wished to be or not. Even the involvement of Cadwgan ab Bleddyn and his brothers in the Bellême rebellion was not without its specifically Welsh context. Just as much as Robert and Arnulf, the sons of Bleddyn will have had their own advantage in mind, seeking to expand their territory and to exploit the disunity of their neighbours. Over the next two centuries, Welsh leaders would repeatedly exploit disturbances within the Norman state to their own benefit. The change of lordship from Arnulf to the king at Pembroke will have caused local disruptions, almost certainly, and these doubtless contributed to the brief rise of Hywel ap Goronwy.

Henry I remained in England until the summer of 1104, but during the rest of 1104 and on into 1105, and for much of 1107, 1108 and 1109, he was frequently absent in Normandy. In south-west Wales, Gerald was thus left increasingly to make his own decisions as to the management and control of the lordship of Pembroke. This is not to say, however, that Henry was uninterested or unaware of what was happening there, or that he was not troubled by the repeated disturbances. As R. R. Davies has pointed out, Wales might not be ignored for strategic reasons: problems there had there, especially problems involving those of his lords who had lands spread out over England and Normandy as well as Wales, as these always had the potential to expand and to provoke further disturbances elsewhere. The ambitions of marcher barons, also, might lead them to lay claim to powers wider than those to which they were entitled.[27] Some time around 1108, Henry decided to introduce a colony of Flemings to Dyfed, seeking through them to help stabilise the area, both by the presence of tenants, minor gentry and farmers who owed their land to him and had no ties to the native nobility, and through the introduction of a new economic impetus.[28] They settled in the Rhos district, the hinterland of Pembroke Castle, and thus will have come under Gerald's purview.

He was not wholly occupied with royal business; however, it appears that while monitoring the political situation and maintaining order amongst the disparate inhabitants of the earldom of Pembroke, Gerald had also found time to expand his own lands. He already possessed Carew, close to the centre of the earldom at Pembroke, but in 1108, he built a castle at Cenarth Bychan, usually identified as Cilgerran, close to the river Teifi and to the harbour at Cardigan. Like Carew, this new castle was sited close to an existing important fortress, the castle at Cardigan, which had been founded by Arnulf de Bellême, and which served as the major defensive nexus for the northern end of the earldom. Like Pembroke, it could dominate both coast and hinterland. It is likely that Gerald may have had responsibilities in the Cardigan region, as well as around Pembroke. Cardigan castle had its own guardian, however, an officer named Stephen. According to the *Brutiau* Gerald:

> ...fortified it [Cilgerran] with ditches and walls and thought to place there for safe keeping his wife and his sons and his wealth and all his valuables.[29]

It should be asked, however, if this was in fact his main intention. Cilgerran lay on the border with the old Welsh kingdom of Ceredigion, the overlordship of which had long been in dispute between the Welsh rulers of Deheubarth, Gwynedd and Powys. By 1108, the Normans formed one more set of claimants in this long conflict. And, in 1108, the dynasty of Powys was very much on the rise. We have seen that, in 1106, Owain ap Cadwgan of Powys had attacked and killed his cousins from the old kingdom of Arwystli. Cadwgan had long laid claim to Ceredigion, and indeed had been confirmed in possession of at least some parts of it in 1099. The de Bellême rebellion had weakened his position and left his two brothers, Iorwerth and Maredudd, in royal prisons. However, in 1107, Maredudd succeeded in escaping, and making his way back to his brother and their lands. He was a loyal brother and ally to Cadwgan, and, moreover, a clever and determined man – he would become prince of Powys in his own right in 1116. On his death in 1132, he was remembered as 'the splendour and defence of the men of Powys'.[30] His return to Powys was a boost to Cadwgan and was to contribute to the events of the next few years. Gerald of Windsor will have known Cadwgan and Maredudd, perhaps through their dealings with Earl Robert, perhaps through his long association with south-west Wales, and he must have had a keen awareness of their abilities and ambitions. That he chose to fortify Cilgerran, to the rear of Cardigan, in that year suggests strongly that he was anticipating an assault from the rulers of Powys upon the earldom. Why did he install Nest and their children in what might become a war zone? The most likely explanation is that he hoped that she might be able to help him in negotiating with Cadwgan, Maredudd and Owain, who were all her kinsmen. It should, however, be born in mind that this section of the vernacular Welsh Chronicles was compiled and probably somewhat revised retrospectively, and that the mention of Nest and her children in this reference to the building of Cilgerran may have been composed in the awareness of what was to transpire in the following year.

The year 1109 was to be a key one in Nest's life, and it is her experiences of that year that were to give rise to her legend as the Helen of Wales. Before this time, such impact as she may have made upon her neighbours and contemporaries was not such as to impel recording. But in 1109, her name enters our extant Welsh historical records, and in a way more reminiscent of the swashbuckling adventures of a Maid Marian than the sober life of a Cambro-Norman married lady. According to the *Brutiau*, Cadwgan ab Bleddyn held a feast in that year for all his nobility and for his kinsmen, notably his eldest son, Owain, who was at that time in Powys. The Welsh Chronicles do not tell us the precise location of the feast, but it seems to have been in the neighbourhood of Cilgerran. Owain, hearing that Nest was at Cilgerran, decided to make a courtesy visit to her, as she was his cousin, and, on doing so, fell in love with her. He gathered a few men together, and, by night, gained entry to the castle by scrambling over the ditch and the wall. His men then proceeded to set fire to the buildings within, to create a distraction, and then surrounded the building in which Nest and Gerald were asleep. Gerald was confused and alarmed by this action, and appealed to Nest for assistance: she persuaded him to escape via a privy hole, and, once he had fled, informed the attackers that he was absent. Owain and his men entered and searched, finding only Nest and four children, whom they seized and carried off, having plundered the stronghold. Cadwgan, on discovering what his son had done, appealed to him to restore both property and captives. Owain released the children, at Nest's request, but refused to listen to his father, provoking a campaign against both himself and his father, involving both Welsh rivals and Norman lords with interests in Wales and its border.

It is an exciting story, but we should hesitate to take it at full face value. In the first place, as I have argued elsewhere, this section of the vernacular Welsh Chronicles shows signs of having been revised or rewritten at some later period to enhance the political standing of the dynasty of Powys and in particular to show the heroism and daring of Owain ap Cadwgan.[31] The account of the abduction of Nest, and the entries for several years on either side, are unusually detailed, including direct speech, giving them the form almost more of a prose tale than of a record of events. This is not to say that they should be discounted in their entirety. But care must be taken in considering the details they offer to us. They are retrospective, but they may well have been composed within the sphere of influence of the royal house of Powys and with access to earlier accounts and perhaps to the memories of those who had viewed the events themselves.[32]

What was going on in 1109? As noted, Cadwgan ab Bleddyn's loyal brother had recently escaped from prison, and with his return it may well be that Cadwgan felt his own position and in particular his ability to recruit and retain support was improved, as he might now call upon those men of the *uchelwyr* who considered themselves allies of Maredudd in person. The *Brutiau* do not tell us why Cadwgan laid on his great feast in 1109, but the prose tales, and also heroic poems such as *Yr Gododdin* suggest that such events often preceded a raid or the opening of a military campaign, and were given by way of an incentive and an encouragement to those men who were about to fight. It is possible that Cadwgan was engaged upon recruiting and rewarding supporters to aid him in an attack on the lands under Gerald's supervision. We hear little of Cadwgan between the end of the de Bellême rebellion in 1102 and 1109. It is likely that in those years, he was engaged upon repairing the damage done to his own power by that rebellion and by the behaviour of his brother Iorwerth, who had abandoned Robert de Bellême in favour of the king, in hope of gaining all of his hereditary lands, and who had instead ended up in prison. We have seen that in 1106, his son Owain had killed two distant kinsmen, the sons of Trahaearn ap Caradog, who probably represented a threat to Cadwgan's lordship. The account of the *Brutiau* between 1109 and 1111 present Cadwgan as rather in awe and fear of Henry I and his power, an interpretation which has sometimes been followed in modern discussion of this period.[33] Yet down to this time, Cadwgan was a leading light – perhaps the leading light – in Welsh resistance to the incursions of the Normans. He instigated and probably co-ordinated the rebellion of the 1090s; he joined the de Bellême rebellion and avoided capture or punishment. His sphere of activity and influence ranged from Tegeingl in the far north-east corner of Wales to Cydweli in the south-west. His allies had included at various times the heir to Gwynedd, the lords of Buellt and the *uchelwyr* of Tegeingl. His family connexions linked him not only to Nest and her brother, Gruffudd ap Rhys, but to the royal house of Gwynedd, the nobility of Dyfed, Buellt and Tegeingl, and even to the Normans of the Shropshire border.[34] As has been noted, he was the heir to a kingship which had extended over much of Wales, certainly including Gwynedd, Powys and Ceredigion, and he seems never to have forgotten this. In 1109, it is very likely that, aided by Maredudd and Owain, he was in the process of rekindling resistance to Norman expansion. An assault on Cilgerran was a logical first step in this process: Cadwgan and his immediate kin seem to have had a particular interest in retaining Ceredigion, and this castle, with its neighbour at Cardigan, represented a strong threat on the border of that territory.[35]

Why, then, would Owain abduct Nest? We cannot wholly discount the claim in the *Brutiau* that Owain was attracted to her – or, indeed, she to him. I would suggest, however, that her abduction was opportunistic, rather than the main object of the attack upon Cilgerran. Such abductions are not unprecedented in medieval Wales: in 1041, the great king Gruffudd ap Llywelyn had carried off the wife of his rival, Hywel ab Edwin, and taken her for his own. Such events are not simply records of rape: they are political acts, serving to undermine the status and honour of the man whose wife is stolen. In kidnapping Nest, Owain delivered a considerable insult to Gerald in both Welsh and Norman eyes. Here was a man who could not protect his own wife. In later years the gesture was to cost Owain dearly, but in 1109, it was a notable triumph.

We know nothing of how Nest felt: the long account of the *Brutiau* gives us few clues – and we cannot be sure of its reliability. If its tale is accepted, then she was a practical woman, who recognised that in the short term Gerald faced more danger than she, and that his freedom was of more value than hers. The advice to Gerald to escape via a privy provides a note of comedy – it may reflect less a real event than an attempt by the compiler or writer of this entry in our chronicles to humiliate Gerald or his descendants. But it is still a clever suggestion: our chronicler found it believable that Nest was quick-thinking, and perhaps we may follow him in this. As to her relations with Owain, it gives us few clues. The chronicles tell us that Owain was infatuated with her, and therefore willing to accede to her request that her children be released and returned to

Gerald. They do not tell us whether she too was restored to her husband. As with the other elements of the text, we must use caution in our interpretation. It appears that the chronicler disapproves of the abduction as a blot on the behaviour of his hero, but his objection is not the modern one of horror at rape. Rather, he writes of diabolic influence leading Owain astray, 'at the instigation of the Devil, he was moved by passion and love for the woman'.[36] It is a monkish response to signs of lust in his hero, and Nest's feelings are not considered relevant to the account. We do not know if Nest loved her husband: we do not know if she liked or disliked Owain ap Cadwgan. It seems very likely that she must have been frightened or alarmed. If we can trust the long description in the *Brutiau* however, she did not lose her head and succeeded in persuading Owain to free her children. As a legend, it appears romantic – the dashing prince carrying off the woman he loved. In reality, we are probably seeing here the brutal outcome of an act of war, in which Nest was more a tool to be used against her husband than a person in her own right.

The *Brutiau* do provide us with one more interesting piece of information here, and that is the list given of the children present at the time of the raid: Owain and his men 'seized Nest and her two sons and the third son, whom Gerald had by a concubine, and a daughter.'[37] Who were these children? To answer this question, we must return to the information supplied to us by Nest's grandson, Gerald of Wales, who does not mention the abduction. In his autobiography he names William fitz Gerald, Robert, Henry, Maurice, William Hay, Hywel, Walter, David, Angharad and Gwladus.[38] It is a long list, and it is certain that not all of those named were children also of Gerald. Henry was Nest's son by Henry I, and Robert was to be fathered by Stephen, Constable of Cardigan after 1109. From other references by Gerald of Wales, we know that William fitz Gerald, Maurice, David and Angharad were all her children with Gerald. William inherited Gerald's Welsh holdings after his death; Maurice was amongst the Norman invaders of Ireland after 1167; David became bishop of St Davids in 1148; Angharad married William, lord of Barri, and became the mother of Gerald of Wales. The remaining names are more troublesome, and we cannot be certain that they are all genuine children of Nest. Crouch has noted that Hywel may be another son by Stephen of Cardigan – he laid claim to one of Stephen's former holdings, Lampeter.[39] William Hay was probably the son of one Hait, who was a Fleming and, in 1130, sheriff of Pembroke: nothing at all is known of the father or fathers of Walter or Gwladus. It should be born in mind that we cannot be certain that Gerald of Wales was correct in this list: he seems never to have met Nest, and may have become confused – some of the children named may have been foster- or step-children. As was noted above, the *Brutiau* tell us of four children in 1109, one of whom is said to be the illegitimate son of Gerald. This may, perhaps, be the same person as the Walter named by Gerald of Wales. It is equally possible, however, that he may have been Henry, Nest's son by Henry I, and that the chronicler has confused his parentage. Crouch considers that Henry fitz Henry was not born before 1114: if he is correct, then the son mentioned here may be Walter or some other child who died young or lived in obscurity. The other three must have been Nest's eldest two sons with Gerald, William and perhaps David – the daughter must be Angharad. None of them can have been very old, and it may be that family memories of this incident were blurred by youthfulness as well as by a desire to protect the reputation of Nest.

Owain's raid on Cilgerran did not long go unavenged. News of what had transpired rapidly reached the king's representative at Shrewsbury, Bishop Richard of London. His first move was to exploit the fractures and factions of native Welsh politics. He summoned Owain's cousins, Madog and Ithel, sons of Rhirid ab Bleddyn, and offered them the lands of Owain and his father Cadwgan, if they could take them. They were joined in this by Llywarch ap Trahaearn, whose brothers had been killed by Owain in 1106, and Uchdryd ab Edwin, the most powerful nobleman of north-east Wales. Their hosts descended on Powys and Ceredigion, causing widespread chaos. Within a short time, Cadwgan and Owain were forced to flee. Owain took ship at Aberdyfi for Ireland and the court of Muirchertach ua Briain, who had sheltered Cadwgan in 1098. Did Owain also hope to meet with or contact his father's former ally, Arnulf de Bellême? It is possible, but it is more likely that he was simply following in the footsteps of all those other Welsh kings of the tenth and eleventh centuries who had turned to Ireland for aid. Cadwgan remained behind in Powys. Uchdryd ab Edwin, with whom he had had dealings before, had prevented widespread looting in Powys and Ceredigion, and it is not impossible that he and Cadwgan had some arrangement or agreement to defuse or undermine Madog and Ithel. Through his marriage to an Norman noblewoman, the daughter of Picot de Sai, one of the marcher lords of Shropshire, Cadwgan possessed land within the Norman realm, and from this base he was able to open negotiations with the king. Madog and Ithel had already proved unsatisfactory: they had quarrelled with each other, adding to the warfare in north-east Wales, and Madog had offended Bishop Richard by refusing to obey his legal dictates. Cadwgan was a serial rebel, it is true, but he was also a known quantity, and he was no longer a young man. Perhaps Henry I and his officers hoped that Cadwgan's desire for conflict might be waning. We do not know their precise reasons, but before the end of the year, Cadwgan was restored in his territories, on payment of a fine of one hundred pounds, and having been made to swear not to give help to Owain.

Where was Nest in all of this? It is very unlikely that Owain would have taken her with him to Ireland. From the account of the *Brutiau*, he had lingered a while in the neighbourhood of Aberdyfi, probably in hiding. Keeping Nest with him – especially if she was an unwilling captive – would have made his situation more precarious and more liable to discovery. We should probably conclude that she remained in Wales. But what became of her? The *Brutiau* does not tell us. There is other information available to us, however. We know that in 1114 her brother, Gruffudd ap Rhys, stayed with Gerald at Pembroke castle. And we know that while in 1109, she and Gerald seemingly had two sons, eventually they had a third, Maurice. We should probably conclude that she returned to Gerald. By 1109, she had spent much of her life amongst the Anglo-Normans, while the courts of the Welsh kings and princes must have reminded her of her childhood, she will have felt equally at home in the keeps of the Normans. There is no reason to believe that she had welcomed Owain's abduction: the *Brutiau* refer to it as a violation. She had been the mistress of Henry I and then Gerald's wife, but we do not know that she was ever willingly unfaithful. She was caught between two worlds: native Welsh and colonial Norman. The assumption that she sought or welcomed sexual adventures depends not on the records we possess but on the misleading myth of the liberated 'Celtic' woman, which, as I have argued earlier in this book, has no basis in eleventh- or twelfth-century reality. It is most likely that she was glad to return to her home, her husband, and perhaps most of all, her children, and that her abduction was, for her, a frightening and painful episode.

Did Gerald welcome her? We can hope so. If we may believe the account of the *Brutiau*, her quick thinking may have saved his life. It is likely that they were soon reconciled: we know they had at least one more child, and we know, too, that Gerald welcomed her brother as a guest. It should be noted, however, that although Gerald of Wales was clearly raised to admire his grandfather, and told tales of his exploits, he is largely silent on the subject of Nest. He mentions her solely as the mother of children and as a scion of a noble lineage. This might, of course, reflect no more than the twelfth-century mind-set, which set little value on women save as vessels for inheritance and the transmission of property. However, it might also suggest a certain reticence in the family on the subject of the colourful Nest. We do know that, however he behaved towards his wife, Gerald neither forgot the incident nor forgave Owain ap Cadwgan.

It is hardly surprising. Owain soon returned from Ireland, and embarked upon a wide-ranging campaign of raiding, plundering and attacking Norman lands. Dyfed, which lay under Gerald's jurisdiction, suffered considerably from this: Owain burnt towns, carried off the inhabitants to be sold into slavery, and stole livestock. The rebellion – for such it soon became – ran on throughout 1110 and into 1111. Various attempts to defuse it by the king and by the Anglo-

Normans in Wales met with little success until, in 1111, Cadwgan ab Bleddyn was murdered by his nephew, Madog ap Rhirid. Madog had at first been an ally of Bishop Richard against Owain, but before the end of 1109, he had joined Owain in rebellion. Their friendship was tenuous, however – as first cousins, each was sharply aware that the other had a strong claim to the rulership of the family lands – and by 1111, they had fallen out. On learning of the murder of his father, Owain ap Cadwgan abandoned any contact with his cousin, and turned instead to Henry I. It appears that, in his eyes, by comparison with his dynastic rival, the Normans were the lesser evil. Henry confirmed him in his father's lands, after Owain gave hostages for his good behaviour. It seems, however, that he continued to make the occasional foray into Norman lands in Wales.

This was not the end of the affair, however. Owain had not forgotten his father's murder, and harboured a desire for revenge. In 1113, he and his uncle Maredudd laid hands on Madog ap Rhirid, who by this time was also within the king's peace. Owain did not kill him: we do not know why. Their kinship will not have been a factor: there are many precedents in medieval Wales for kin slaying. For whatever reason, Owain chose to blind Madog instead, and deprived him of his lands. This took place far from Cilgerran and Pembroke, but the ramifications of the long conflict will have affected Nest and her family. Gerald must have been away frequently, defending vulnerable lands or pursuing the rebels. The plundering in Dyfed may have led to a shortage of foodstuffs and to the disruption of trade and travel. In additional to all this, Nest may have faced suspicion or hostility from amongst the Anglo-Norman and Flemish communities. She was, after all, Welsh, and a cousin to the rebels.

By 1114, Henry I had had enough. He came to Wales with an army, determined to put a stop to the chaos and to end the raiding activities not only of Owain, but of his northern neighbour, Gruffudd ap Cynan, who had been slowly chipping away at the north Welsh lands of the earl of Chester. On arriving in Wales, Henry summoned to him the Norman forces of the whole country, which will have included Gerald. Did Nest accompany Gerald? It is unlikely that she would go with him on a campaign. If she met with Henry 1114, it would have been at one of the Norman castles in Wales. As a woman, she had no place in an army, and Henry will have had men in his forces who could act as translators. It seems to me likely that she remained at one of her husband's castles. It had probably been a good number of years since she had been Henry's mistress. She cannot have expected him to have time for her on a campaign, nor would it have been courteous towards her husband for her to endeavour to see her former lover. It is sometimes argued that Henry's affair with Nest must have taken place in 1114, but for the reasons given above, it seems to me to be unlikely.[40] In addition, it must be asked if Henry would have had time for an affair – or if he would have wanted potentially to endanger the loyalty to him of a man who, by now, possessed considerable influence and power in south-west Wales.

In the end, there were no pitched battles between Norman and Welsh forces. Instead, Owain, Gruffudd ap Cynan and their allies elected to come to terms with Henry. This time, the peace held. It seems that Owain had at last received what he desired – the peaceful possession of his hereditary lands.[41] Thereafter, Owain was to remain on goods terms with the king – if not always with his representatives in Wales.

The peace marked the end of the rebellion, but it was not the end of Nest's associations with rebels. In 1093, after the death of their father, the elder of her two brothers, Gruffudd ap Rhys, had been taken for safety to Ireland. He must have been still a child – perhaps a young one – at that time, and he had remained in Ireland throughout the rest of his childhood and into young manhood. But in around 1113, he returned to Wales, 'And there he stayed for about two years with his kinsmen, a part thereof with Gerald, the officer of Pembroke castle … for the latter's wife was Nest, daughter of Rhys, a sister to the said young man …'[42]

It is hard to guess what Gruffudd was expecting on his return. During the long years of his exile, there had been substantial changes in his homeland, and where his father had once had *llysoedd* stood Norman castles and Flemish settlements. Of the Welshmen who had occupied positions of power when he was a child, only the devious and unreliable Uchdryd ab Edwin remained. Gruffudd's uncle, Rhydderch ap Tewdwr, was a solid supporter of the Normans, perhaps a result of Nest's marriage to Gerald. It had been more than twenty years since Gruffudd had been sent from Wales. He will have heard news from his homeland, via traders or fellow exiles, and perhaps some of his father's former followers had stayed with him in Ireland, to ensure he continued to speak Welsh and remembered his heritage. It may be that the news of Owain's rebellion and the ensuing chaos had tempted him to return and join the rebels. Or it may have been the ending of that same rebellion which brought him: he may have hoped to benefit from its consequences. Perhaps he looked to his sister and her husband to establish him. There are many possibilities. It seems likely that at first he simply remained with his kin, acclimatising back to Deheubarth and trying to build for himself a network of friends and contacts. Apparently, he made no attempt to see the king, or to make any form of official claim to his father's lands, but by the very fact of staying with Gerald at Pembroke, he had made his presence known to the Norman colonists.

To some of the Welsh of Deheubarth, he must have represented a new hope or focus for nationalistic ideas.[43] But to others – Welsh as well as Norman and Flemings – he must have appeared as a threat to social and political order. Many of the nobles who had followed Rhys ap Tewdwr will have died and others will have found new lords. Some, like Rhydderch ap Tewdwr, had carved out for themselves a role in the new, mixed Cambro-Norman culture. As Babcock has noted, the twenty years since 1093 had wrought considerable changes in the structure of native Welsh society.[44] Gruffudd must rapidly have realised that he occupied an awkward position. Within two years of his return, according to the Welsh Chronicles, Gruffudd found himself accused of fomenting rebellion against Henry I.[45] It is not at all clear if the accusation was true. As has been mentioned, Gruffudd was a threat simply in himself. We know that he did not remain with his sister all the time: according to the *Brutiau* he also stayed with friends, sometimes secretly. His furtiveness may have been a product of his sensitive situation, but it certainly had a suspicious appearance. On learning of the accusation against him, he fled north, to the lands of Gruffudd ap Cynan, which had the lowest density of Norman settlers.[46] This perhaps shows his political naivety: Gruffudd ap Cynan had been king of Gwynedd since 1099, and had probably been slowly expanding his sphere of influence, but he had, since becoming king, taken care never to attract overmuch attention from the Normans or from Henry I. He had been only peripherally involved in the upheavals of 1109–1114, but he seems to have taken careful note of the scale of the resources available to Henry. He was not willing to be compromised by sheltering Gruffudd ap Rhys, and within a very short time he undertook to betray the latter to the Normans. This action was not universally popular amongst the *uchelwyr* of Gwynedd. Someone warned Gruffudd ap Rhys of the danger, and he fled to sanctuary at the church of Aberdaron, before making his way back to Deheubarth. He may not have intended rebellion, but this adventure defined his course for him. He was met in Ystrad Tywi by men anxious to support him and to resist the Normans, and with them, he began attacking Norman and Flemish settlements.

It was probably the last thing his sister had wanted to see. More than ever, she found herself caught between her two cultures. Gruffudd may have been a near stranger to her when he first returned, but she must have come to know him well over the first two years of his return. Their other brother, Hywel, had long been imprisoned in one of the former strongholds of Arnulf de Bellême, where Nest may have been able to see him. In 1115, he escaped and joined Gruffudd ap Rhys. Did Nest help him? It must be a possibility. At the same time, she will have known that any uprising on behalf of her brothers would lead to reprisals, and that her husband would be obliged to lead some of the forces against him. Her home and its surrounding lands were in danger of further attacks. One or other of Gruffudd and Gerald – or both – could well be killed. The rebellion, if it proved initially successful, might spread, plunging Wales once more into years of conflict and violence. Perhaps she tried to persuade her brother to back down or to make peace. We do not know. In 1116, Gruffudd's raids became a concerted campaign. He and his followers attacked the castles of Arberth, Llandovery, Swansea, Carmarthen, and Aberystwyth, amongst others.[47] His support from the Welsh was not uniform: a number of the *uchelwyr*, including Rhydderch ap Tewdwr, supported the Normans, assisting in the defence of various strongholds and settlements.[48] One perhaps surprising ally of the Normans was Owain ap Cadwgan. It might at first seem strange for Owain to fight against a Welsh rebellion. However, it must be noted that much of Gruffudd ap Rhys' activities had occurred in or near Ceredigion, a territory it seems he hoped to gain for himself. This would not have suited Owain at all, as he, too, had a hereditary claim to that land, and he did not wish to surrender it. By supporting the Normans, moreover, he gained the goodwill of Henry I and thus increased his chances of having his own claims to various lands upheld.

Gerald, naturally, was closely involved in the campaign against his brother-in-law. His own position was probably delicate: he had, after all, given hospitality to Gruffudd over a long period. But he placed his duty first. At some point in 1116, he found himself near Carmarthen with an army of Flemish settlers. They came upon another army, lead by Owain, which had been fighting in the neighbourhood.[49] The *Brutiau* tell us that:

> ...the Flemings ... were fired with the old hate that formerly existed between them and Owain; for many a time had Owain done them hurt. Instigated also by Gerald, the man from whom Owain had carried off his wife, and whose castle he had burned, and whose spoil he had carried off, they thought to pursue Owain ... And then he [Owain] attacked them boldly, and they [the Flemings] too stood manfully; and with shooting on either side, Owain was wounded until he was slain.[50]

Gerald had finally had his revenge for the insult of 1109. He had also weakened the Welsh of Powys and Ceredigion, at least for a time. From his point of view, it was a satisfactory outcome. We do not know what Nest thought: she may have had other concerns. The

147

wider conflict had turned against her brother Gruffudd, and he was in hiding somewhere in Ystrad Tywi. The death of Owain led to upheavals in north-east Wales,[51] and by the end of 1116, the danger of Welsh rebellion seems to have been defused. Gerald returned to Nest, content in his revenge.

Gruffudd ap Rhys seems to have remained in hiding for some time following his defeat near Aberystwyth, and it is likely that Nest did not know his whereabouts. He may not have wished to risk her husband finding out: indeed, he may not have trusted Nest herself. Perhaps some of his erstwhile supporters sheltered him, perhaps he spent some time in Ireland. But at some point over the next few years, he came to terms with the Normans, and was granted a small territory – the cantref of Caeo – by Henry I. It is tempting to speculate that Nest had something to do with this. Perhaps she worked on her husband to make peace with Gruffudd, in his person as royal representative in south-west Wales.

Gruffudd ap Rhys was to live out most of the rest of his life as a minor landholder, overshadowed by the powerful Norman lords who had settled throughout south Wales, and, perhaps, dependent upon the good auspices of his sister to keep him out of too much trouble. It is unclear if he had ever sought to cause conflict in the first place. As the son of Rhys ap Tewdwr, he was a natural figurehead for those elements within southern Welsh society who sought to throw off Norman rule. As a young man he may have harboured hopes of achieving some level of independence – freeing northern Deheubarth, perhaps, or gaining control of Ceredigion – and thus of maintaining at least some of the status and powers of his father. But he was never to join the ranks of the Welsh princes and kings. Unlike Gruffudd ap Cynan in Gwynedd, or Cadwgan, Owain, and, after them, Maredudd ab Bleddyn in Powys, Gruffudd ap Rhys was unable to restore any part of the sovereignty of Deheubarth. That task was to wait for his son, Rhys ap Gruffudd, better known as the Lord Rhys, who was to rebuild southern Welsh power during the second half of the twelfth century.[52] But Gruffudd was never able to escape the consequences of his birth. In 1127, by which time he was settled in his lands of Caeo and married with children, he found himself once more the object of suspicion and was expelled from his holdings by order of the king. Was he complicit in some plot against Norman rule? The *Brutiau* claim not, stating rather that his Norman neighbours had concocted lies about him.[53] But whoever authored this section in our chronicles clearly sympathised with Gruffudd, and might have wished to hide or elide any action of his which might incur censure. Perhaps once again Nest acted as intermediary for her brother, for he seems later on to have been restored again to his property. We do not know exactly when he returned to his lands, only that it must have been before 1136.

By the latter year, Nest had been widowed. Gerald vanishes from our records after the killing of Owain ap Cadwgan in 1116. We do not know when he died, or how, but it must have occurred before 1136, and probably before 1130. In 1130, it was Hait, the sheriff, who accounted for Pembroke, and not Gerald, suggesting that the latter not longer held power there.[54] In 1133, Gilbert de Clare was made earl of Pembroke. In principle, a man of Gerald's rank might serve under an earl – as, indeed, he had under Arnulf de Bellême at the start of his career. But in practice, by 1133, if Gerald was still alive, he must have been an old man. His first recorded action occurred in 1093, when he became Arnulf's castellan. To occupy such a position, he must have been fully adult and reasonably well seasoned in battle: in the circumstances of that place and time, such a post might not safely be given to a very young or very inexperienced man. By 1136, when a new Welsh rebellion broke out on the death of Henry I, it was Gerald's sons, and not Gerald, who were amongst the Norman forces. It is likely that Gerald was dead, and, indeed, that he had died some years before.

What of Nest? Her situation, on widowhood, cannot have been comfortable. We do not know what, if any, dower arrangements had been made for her upon her marriage, but, as a daughter of Rhys ap Tewdwr, she remained a potential heiress, and, once unmarried, a potential cause of trouble. Under Welsh law, she could turn to her sons for support, but Norman practice differed. A women with lands, titles or a significant claim to inheritance could not expect to remain long unmarried. By this time, Nest must have been securely part of the social landscape of Cambro-Norman Wales. There would have been only two real choices open to her: remarriage, or entering a convent. We know nothing of her attitude to religion, but Wales had no tradition of convents at that time. Becoming a nun would have meant leaving Wales, which she might well not have wished to do. Pressure may have been brought upon her to remarry fairly quickly, especially as it seems that she was still of childbearing age – and famously beautiful.

Later writers have been hard on Nest, and it is often implied that, aside from her children with Gerald, that her other offspring must have been illegitimate. The basis for this seems to be her known liaison with Henry I and her abduction by Owain ap Cadwgan.[55] But to be the mistress of a king was a very different thing than to be that of a sheriff or a minor lord. It has been shown how a liaison with a royal prince could bring considerable advantage to the family of a young woman, and it is quite possible that some of the women with whom Henry had relationships may have been pushed into it by their kinsmen. Nest, as an orphan and a captive, may have seen Henry as a means to escape her situation or to achieve some kind of status of her own. As regards Owain, we have no reason to believe she colluded in any way in her own abduction. Widowhood did not convey any special protection in Anglo-Norman England or in Wales.[56] If she did not wish to become a nun, Nest probably had to remarry – and not necessarily through her own choice and in her own time. Given that we do not hear of her sons acting in the military sphere until 1136, they may have still been minors or only newly adult when their father died. They would thus be in no position to protect Nest. Her brother Gruffudd had shown himself to have a talent for trouble, rather than one for diplomacy or negotiation. Was his expulsion in 1127 connected to Nest? It cannot be proved, but it is tempting to speculate that she had been widowed around this time and had taken shelter with him, to the displeasure of a would-be suitor. Who might this have been? The most likely candidate is

Hait, the sheriff of Pembroke. According to Gerald of Wales, Nest had at least one son with him. He would have been familiar with her, for, as one of the leaders of the Flemish settlers in south-west Wales, he would have had regular contact with Gerald and his household. If he was an ambitious man, marriage to the widow of his former overlord would mark a step up the social ladder, and might even lead to his acquiring Gerald's former position as the king's officer. If he did marry Nest soon after Gerald's death, however, he never climbed higher than sheriff, and the marriage may have been short-lived. Neither he, nor his apparent son William, make much of an appearance in our records.

In the second half of the twelfth century, two of Nest's sons were to play significant roles in the Norman invasion and colonisation of Ireland. One of these was Maurice, lord of Llanstephan, probably her second son by Gerald. The other was Robert fitz Stephen.

Robert's father was Stephen, constable of Cardigan castle. Nest's home of Cilgerran castle lay close to Cardigan, and Stephen may well have been a familiar figure during the years of her marriage to Gerald. We do not know when he became constable – he is first noted in that office in 1136, leading the Norman forces against a Welsh attack. He probably also possessed lands in Cemais – certainly, his son Robert did – and it is very possible that he owed his position and rise to the patronage of Gerald. He must have been younger than Gerald, and probably also than Nest. In 1136, he rode alongside her sons by Gerald, now adult fighting men under his command. Stephen may have been much in the same mould as Gerald: a servant of the king, owing rank and position to patronage and offering loyalty in return. His household, probably mixed Norman and Welsh, would have seemed familiar to Nest – more so than the Flemish environment of Hait the sheriff. Her son with Stephen, Robert, was probably the youngest of her children, perhaps up to twenty years younger than Henry fitz Henry, her son by the king. By 1145, Robert seems to have succeeded his father as castellan, a job he held effectively, and in 1157, we find him aiding Henry II on campaign in Gwynedd. Unlike the shadowy William Hay, Robert was a fully integrated member of Nest's family. In later life, he was a close associate of Maurice fitz Gerald and the sons of William fitz Gerald: he was well known, too, to his nephew Gerald of Wales, who admired him, describing him as 'a unique example of courage and true endurance … a well-built and sturdy man, and handsome, a man who lived well, generous and of an open and cheerful disposition'.[57] We do not know when he was born, but he died in around 1183, as Lord of Cork in Ireland. By this time, he must have been in his fifties, at the lowest estimate, suggesting he was born no later than about 1130.

The marriage to Hait may have been a result of necessity or even force. However, it is likely that in marrying Stephen, Nest made her own choice, or, at least, one which met with the full approval of her family. Robert apparently grew up in close connexion to his elder brothers, the sons of Gerald, and with their sons, who became his allies and associates in the invasion of Ireland. We may hope that this last relationship was a happy one.

Even in later life, however, Nest remained caught between two worlds. Her former lover, Henry I, died on 1 December 1135 in Normandy. He had no legitimate son, and many of his barons were loath to accept his daughter, Matilda, as ruler of England. The troubles and conflicts which arose in England and Normandy provided an opportunity for the Welsh to rebel once again and attempt to expel the Norman invaders. Rebellion broke out in 1136, spearheaded by Owain and Cadwaladr, sons of Gruffudd ap Cynan. They swept south, ravaging and raising throughout Ceredigion. Nest's home, now at Cardigan, and her former home at Cilgerran lay in the path of danger. Stephen marshalled his forces to meet the Welsh, accompanied by Nest's sons by Gerald. Nest had long experience of watching the men of her family ride to war. Gerald himself had always come back, but her father had not, and she must have feared for her new husband and her sons.

She may have feared also for her brother. Gruffudd ap Rhys had joined with the forces from Gwynedd to battle against the Normans under his own brother-in-law and nephews. The two sides met between the mouths of the Neath and of the Dyfi, and the Norman side was put to flight. This was not the end of the conflict, however: we know that in the same year further fighting occurred in the vicinity of Kidwelly castle. The local Norman overlord was Maurice of London, who brought an army against the rebellious Gruffudd ap Rhys. But Gruffudd was absent, with the sons of Gruffudd ap Cynan to the north. In his place, Maurice found an army led by Gruffudd's wife, Gwenllian and two of their sons, Morgan and Maelgwn. The incident became another legend in the fitz Gerald family. Gerald of Wales wrote that, 'the princess Gwenllian rode forward at the head of an army, like some second Penthesilea, Queen of the Amazons.'[58] She was Nest's sister-in-law, and, like Nest, the daughter of a Welsh king – Gruffudd ap Cynan of Gwynedd. Unlike Nest, however, she was not caught between the two sides. Her husband and her brothers were allies against the Normans, and her father had been able to retain at least some of his lands throughout her childhood. She lived in a largely Welsh world, removed from the contradictions which had confronted Nest. Her courage impressed Gerald, whose great-aunt she was, but it cost her her life, along with that of her son Morgan. Within a year, Gruffudd ap Rhys too was dead. We do not know the cause of his death: perhaps illness, perhaps wounds. He left young sons, but it is unlikely that Nest had much contact with them, as the rebellion was continuing and they were firmly associated with the nationalist cause. With Gruffudd's death, Nest lost her last close link to the native society of her birth. But it seems that she never forgot that she had been born Welsh. Three of her children bore Welsh names – Angharad, Gwladus and Hywel – and her grandson Gerald of Wales retained a strong sense of his own Welsh ancestry and connexions, doubtless partly instilled in him by his mother Angharad, who will have had a similar experience with her own mother. Daughters did not usually lead armies or diplomatic missions: Angharad and Gwladus were probably the closest to Nest of all her children, growing up in her sphere of the domestic. It is to them that the traditions of her Welsh royal blood will have been particularly transmitted. Yet her sons, too, were aware of it: the eldest, Henry, gave his own son the Welsh name Meilyr.

Another of her grandsons bore the name Gruffudd, perhaps after her brother.[59]

We do not know when she died: her life is recorded only thinly and by and large in relation to men. Her last years may have been turbulent, as rebellion continued and the Norman colonists received some serious defeats. Ceredigion saw a large portion of the fighting: it is likely she retreated back into the safer environs of Pembroke, under the protection of her sons, as well as her husband. As a child, she cannot have imagined that her life would turn out as it did. Her expectation was probably marriage to an ally or vassal of her father's, and a home very like the one in which she was born. But circumstances brought her instead into the new world of Norman colonists, castles, knights and English royal courts, and made her the ancestress of a dynamic and adventurous dynasty.

NOTES

1 Gerald of Wales, trans. Thorpe, Lewis, *The Journey through Wales / The Description of Wales* (Harmondsworth, 1978), *Journey* book 1, ch.12, p.151; Cambrensis, Giraldi, *Opera*, eds Brewer, J. S., Dimock, J. S., and Warner, G. F., 8 vols (London 1861–91), vol.6, p.93

2 On these rulers, see Maund, K. L., *The Welsh Kings: the medieval rulers of Wales* (Stroud, 2000), pp.46–59.

3 The issue of gender roles will be looked at in more detail in Chapter 2.

4 On royal renders, see Davies, W., *Wales in the Early Middle Ages* (Leicester, 1982), pp.43–47; Charles-Edwards, T. M., 'Food, Drink and Clothing in the Laws of Court' in Charles-Edwards, T. M., Owen, Morfydd E. and Russell, Paul, eds, *The Welsh King and His Court* (Cardiff, 2000), 319–337, pp.321–2.

5 For the hill forts and other early elite sites, see Alcock, L., *Dinas Powys – An Iron Age, Dark Age and Early Medieval Settlement in Glamorgan* (Cardiff, 1963); Alcock, L., *Economy, Society and Warfare among the Britons and Saxons* (Cardiff, 1987); Dark, K. R., *Civitas to Kingdom: British Political Continuity 300–800* (Leicester, 1994).

6 Alcock, L., *Economy*, pp.20–150.

7 This is mentioned by the D and E texts of the *Anglo-Saxon Chronicle* s.a. 1063; Swanton, M., trans. and ed., *The Anglo-Saxon Chronicle* (London, 1996) and by the *Chronicle* of John of Worcester s.a. 1063 and 1064; John of Worcester, *Chronicle* eds and trans., Darlington, R. R., Bray, J., and McGurk, P., (Oxford, 1995–8).

8 Evans, D. S., ed., *Historia Gruffud vab Kenan* (Cardiff, 1977), p.30.

9 Gerald, *Journey,* book 1, chapter 10, trans. Thorpe p.139; *Opera* vol.6, p.80.

10 Edwards, Nancy, 'Landscape and Settlement in Medieval Wales: an Introduction', in Nancy Edwards and Alan Lane, eds *Landscape and Settlement in Medieval Wales* (Oxford, 1997), 1–11, p.9.

11 See previous note.

12 Gantz, J., trans., *The Mabinogion* (Harmondsworth, 1976), pp.59–62, 100.

13 Johnstone, N., 'The Location of the Royal Courts of Thirteenth Century Gwynedd', in Edwards and Lane, eds, *Landscape*, pp.55–69, pp.63–7.

14 Johnstone, N., 'Location', p.67.

15 Gantz, *Mabinogion*, p.55.

16 Gerald, *Description*, book 1, ch.10 trans. Thorpe, p.236; *Opera*, vol.6, p.183.

17 Gantz, *Mabinogion*, p.139.

18 Jenkins, Dafydd , *The Law of Hywel Dda* (Llandysul, 1990), pp.9–12, p.14, p.16, pp.18–21, pp.23–32.

19 Gantz, *Mabinogion*, p.59. The biography of Rhys and Nest's contemporary Gruffudd ap Cynan also makes mention of the significance of generosity in queens, in its description of Gruffudd's wife, Angharad ferch Owain. This text, however, was probably composed in the late twelfth century, and cannot be relied upon as an accurate representation of late eleventh-century customs and behaviour. Evans, D. S., ed. and trans., *A Medieval Prince of Wales The Life of Gruffudd ap Cynan* (Llanerch, 1990), p.42, p.74.

20 Dafydd ab Owain, prince of Gwynedd in the later twelfth century, married Emma of Anjou, an illegitimate daughter of Henry II, while his nephew Llywelyn ap Iorwerth (Llywelyn the Great,

1197–1240) married King John's illegitimate daughter Joanna in the first years of the thirteenth century.

21 Gantz, *Mabinogion*, pp.86–7.

22 There seems to be a dearth of evidence, however, on the production of cloth and clothing. Did Welsh noblewomen spin, weave and sew? It seems likely that they must have, but the evidence is wanting. According to the laws of court, kings and queens made gifts of woollen and linen garments to their household: these must have been made somehow. It is probable that at least some of this work was carried out, if not by the kings' wives and daughters, but by their maids, and daughters must surely have been taught to sew and embroider.

23 Davies, *Wales*, pp.49–50.

24 In the north, Anglesey provided Gwynedd with valuable arable land, while Morgannwg benefited from the lowlands of the Severn valley. However, almost all the best cultivable land in Wales was vulnerable to external attack – Dyfed and Anglesey from sea-going raiders from Ireland or Scandinavia, the border zone from Anglo-Saxon or Anglo-Norman incursions.

25 Gerald, *Description*, book 1, ch.8, trans. Thorpe, p.233; *Opera* vol.6, p.179.

26 Gantz, *Mabinogion*, p.91; Jenkins, *Law*, p.128

27 Jenkins, *Law*, p.180.

28 Jenkins, *Law*, p.176.

29 Gantz, *Mabinogion*, p.74.

30 Gantz, *Mabinogion*, p.91.

31 Alcock, *Dinas Powys*, pp.39–40.

32 Gerald, *Description*, book 1 chapter 6, trans. Thorpe, p.230; *Opera*, vol.6, p.176.

33 Jones, T., trans., *Brut y Tywysogion or the Chronicle of the Princes, Peniarth MS 20 Version* (Cardiff, 1952) [690–689], [986–987]; Jones, T., ed. & trans., *Brut y Tywysogion or the Chronicle of the Princes, Red Book of Hergest Version* (2nd edition Cardiff, 1973) [690–689]; Jones, T., ed. & trans., *Brenhinedd y Saesson, or The Kings of the Saxons* (Cardiff, 1971) [688–689].

34 Gerald, *Description*, book 1 chap 8, trans. Thorpe, p. 233; *Opera*, vol. 6, pp. 179–80.

35 Charles-Edwards et al., *The Welsh King*, pp. 498–9.

36 Gerald, *Description*, book 1 ch. 5, trans. Thorpe, p. 226; *Opera*, vol. 6, p. 172.

37 Evans, *A Medieval Prince*, p. 50, p. 81.

38 Koch, J. T., ed. and trans. *The Gododdin of Aneirin Text and Context from Dark Age Britain* (Cardiff, 1997), pp. 12–13.

39 Charles-Edwards et al., *The Welsh King* pp. 484–5.

40 Charles-Edwards et al., *The Welsh King*, pp. 514–5.

41 Charles-Edwards et al., *The Welsh King*, pp. 520–1.

42 Charles-Edwards et al., *The Welsh King*, pp. 522–3.

43 Davies, *Wales*, p. 49.

44 See the reports by Mark Redknapp in *Archaeology in Wales* vol. 35, (1995), pp. 58–9; vol. 36 (1996), 81–2; vol. 37 (1997), pp. 94–6.

45 The literature on the Vikings is vast, but a good recent starting place is Sawyer, P., ed., *The Oxford Illustrated History of the Vikings* (Oxford, 1997). Roesdahl, E., *The Vikings* (Harmondsworth, 1987) is also useful.

46 The question as to how Welsh leaders like Rhys communicated with these Hiberno-Scandinavian mercenaries is largely unexamined. While occasional Welsh rulers, like Gruffudd ap Cynan and Gruffudd ap Rhys, who were both raised in Ireland, must have spoken the language of their Hiberno-Scandinavian hosts, we do not know if Rhys spoke any language other than Welsh. His communications with William I the Conqueror seem to have occurred at St Davids and were thus probably conducted with clerics using Latin as a *lingua franca*. It is possible, given the amount of Hiberno-Scandinavian contact with Wales in the eleventh century that at least some of the mercenaries spoke some Welsh.

47 *Domesday Book* Herefordshire, fos 187ra and 187va; see also Maund, K. L., *Ireland, Wales and England in the Eleventh Century* (Woodbridge, 1990), p. 29, p. 40.

48 Frederick C. Suppe, 'Who was Rhys Sais: some comments on Anglo-Welsh Relations before 1066', *Haskins Society Journal* 7 (1995), pp. 63–75.

49 On Aelfgar, see Maund, K. L., 'The Welsh Alliances of Earl Aelfgar of Mercia and his Family in the mid-eleventh century', *Anglo-Norman Studies* 11 (1988), pp.181–90.

50 On this, see Grabowski, K., and Dumville, D. N., *Chronicles and Annals of Mediaeval Ireland and Wales* (Woodbridge, 1984).

51 On Sulien, see Lloyd, *A History*, vol.II, pp.459–61.

52 Bede, *A History of the English Church and People* trans. Leo Sherley-Price (Harmondsworth, 1955, rev. ed. 1965), book I, ch.29; book II, ch.2, ch.4; book IV, ch.28.

53 Gildas, *The Ruin of Britain and other documents* ed. and trans. Winterbottom, M., (Chichester, 1978), ch.27–36.

54 This did not become a firm requirement for priests in England, until 1125.

55 An example of this would be Bishop Sulien of St Davids (1072/3–1078 and 1080–1085) and his four sons: see Lloyd, *A History* II, pp.159–161.

56 Ideas of the survival of ancient pre-Christian practices amongst the early medieval Welsh cannot be substantiated from the extant sources.

57 On this Nest, see Maund, K. L., *Ireland*, pp.137–8.

58 Women bearing the name Angharad contemporary or near contemporary with Nest include Angharad ferch Maredudd ap Owain, mother of Gruffudd ap Llywelyn (d.*c.*1064) and his half brothers Bleddyn (d.1075) and Rhiwallon (d.1069), sons of Cynfyn, and Angharad ferch Owain, the wife of Gruffudd ap Cynan (d.1137).

59 Nest's brother Gruffudd (d.1137) married Gwenllian ferch Gruffudd ap Cynan. Nest's mother was named Gwladus, the meaning of which is uncertain.

60 Apart from Nest, the only other Welsh female name with an overt Christian meaning we meet in the eleventh- or twelfth-century sections of the Welsh Chronicles is Cristin. This does not, however, mean that references to faith were uncommon: Welsh royal lines tended to be conservative in their selection of personal names, with particular names being favoured by particular families. Thus, the royal line

of Deheubarth favoured the names Rhys, Gruffudd, Maredudd and Hywel; and the house of Gwynedd shows a preference for Gruffudd, Llywelyn, Owain and Dafydd. As far as female names go, Gwenllian and Angharad are both very popular with all the royal lines (Gruffudd ap Cynan may have had two daughters named Gwenllian): we also find Gwladus, Nest and Elen – the latter also having a Christian context, from Helena, the reputed finder of the Cross. Even where a king or prince married a non-Welsh bride, the name selection remains narrow, and innovative or foreign names are generally not found.

61 This family is sometimes also known as the Second Dynasty of Gwynedd, or the southern branch of the Dynasty of Rhodri Mawr.

62 Gerald, *Description*, book 1, ch.3, trans. Thorpe p.222; *Opera*, vol.6, p.167.

63 For a discussion, see Maund, K. L., *Welsh Kings*, pp.37–9.

64 It is also responsible for a tendency amongst some historians to assume that such a right was inherent in the kingship of England.

65 The degree to which he actually bears any responsibility for the consolidation, promulgation and creation of the Welsh laws is much debated. See Pryce, H., 'The Prologues to the Welsh Law Books', *BBCS* 33 (1986), pp.151–87; Goronwy Edwards, J., 'Hywel Dda and the Welsh Lawbooks', in Dafydd Jenkins, ed., *Celtic Law Papers* (Brussels, 1973), pp.135–60.

66 See Kirby, D. P., 'Hywel Dda: Anglophil?', *Welsh History Review* 8 (1976–7), 1–13, pp.9–10.

67 See Maund, K. L., *Welsh Kings,* pp.53–4.

68 See Maund, K. L., *Welsh Kings*, pp.53–5 pp.57–9; Lloyd, *A History* I, pp.344–6; David E. Thornton, 'Maredudd ab Owain: Most Famous King of the Welsh', *Welsh History Review* 18 (1997), pp.567–91; Davies, W., *Patterns of Power in Early Wales* (Oxford, 1990), p.57.

69 For a modern re-assessment of Maredudd, see especially Thornton, 'Maredudd'.

70 He may have been his father's junior co-ruler, or he may have been *penteulu* of the royal warband. See Maund, K. L., *Welsh Kings*, p.54.

71 Thornton, 'Maredudd', pp.582–5.

72 But not by daughters, sisters, aunts or female cousins. Female rule was not acceptable in medieval Wales.

73 It should be noted, however, that the Welsh Chronicles note Cadwallon's death after their notice of Edwin's invasion. *ByT* (Pen. 20) [991–992]; *ByT* (RB) [990–992]; *BS* [991–992].

74 On the problems of Welsh royal inheritance, see Maund, K. L., 'Dynastic Segmentation and Gwynedd *c*.950–*c*.1000', *Studia Celtica* 32 (1998), pp.155–67; Charles-Edwards, T. M., *Early Irish and Welsh Kinship* (Oxford, 1993), pp.216–25.

75 For a full discussion of Llywelyn, see Maund, K. L., *Welsh Kings*, pp.60–1; Maund, K. L., *Ireland*, pp.59–62.

76 On Rhydderch, see Maund, K. L., *Welsh Kings*, pp.61–2; Maund, K. L., *Ireland*, pp.20–2.

77 See Maund, K. L., *Welsh Kings*, pp.62–4; Maund, K. L., *Ireland*, pp.22–5; Lloyd, *A History*, II, pp.360–1.

78 On Gruffudd ap Rhydderch, see Maund, K. L., *Welsh Kings*, pp.64–5; Maund, K. L., *Ireland*, pp.25–9; Lloyd, *A History*, II, pp.361–3.

79 Alfred the Great had given support to several of the southern Welsh kings against the sons of Rhodri Mawr in the late ninth century.

80 On Gruffudd ap Llywelyn, see Maund, K. L., *Welsh Kings*, pp.63–70; Maund, K. L., *Ireland*, pp.64–70, pp.126–40; Lloyd, *A History* II, pp.357–371.

81 Walter Map, *De Nugis Curialium: Courtiers' Trifles*, eds and trans. James, M. R., Brooke, C. N. L., and Mynors, R. A. B., (Oxford, 1983), pp.186–90. Walter refers to Gruffudd as 'Llywelyn', but it's clear from context that Gruffudd ap Llywelyn is intended.

82 *ByT* (Pen. 20) [1037–1039], [1061–1063]; *ByT* (RB) [–1039], [1060–1063]; *BS* [1037–1039]. At Gruffudd's death, the latter describes him as 'golden-torqued king of the Welsh and their defender' [1061–1063].

83 According to his biographer, when Gruffudd ap Cynan first came to Gwynedd, a wise woman presented him with garments

made from the mantle of Gruffudd ap Llywelyn. Evans, *A Medieval Prince*, p.29, p.60.

84 This was Gruffudd ap Cynan, whose grandfather Iago ab Idwal was the king Gruffudd ap Llywelyn killed to make himself ruler of Gwynedd in 1039.

85 His son, Gruffudd ap Rhys, would be taken to Ireland for refuge after Rhys' death.

86 *ByT* (Pen. 20) [1076–1078].

87 Rhiwallon had been killed in battle in 1069.

88 On Bleddyn and Edwin, see Maund, K. L., 'The Welsh Alliances'.

89 Robert S. Babcock, 'Rhys ap Tewdwr, King of Deheubarth', *Anglo-Norman Studies* 16 (1993), pp.21–35, p.23 has drawn similar conclusions, suggesting that both Cadell and Tewdwr may never have aspired to any rank higher than that of royal warrior.

90 This Cynan was probably the brother of Llywelyn ap Seisyll.

91 Carr, A. D., '*Teulu* and *Penteulu*', in Charles-Edwards et al., *The Welsh Kings*, pp.63–81, p.73.

92 Maredudd was killed in 1035 in battle with the sons of Cynan.

93 One can usefully compare the early career of Gruffudd ap Cynan, king of Gwynedd 1099–1137, here. Gruffudd was certainly brought up and probably born in Ireland, and although his grandfather Iago ab Idwal had ruled Gwynedd between perhaps 1022 and 1039, Gruffudd himself was an unknown quantity. He had considerable difficulty gaining the trust and reliable support of the *uchelwyr*, many of whom preferred his rival, Trahaearn ap Caradog – not a member of the royal house of Gwynedd, but a known and familiar leader. The Welsh Chronicles initially refer to him not as Gruffudd ap [son of] Cynan but Gruffudd grandson of Iago, suggesting that confirming his identity was a significant issue for him. His close associations with Viking bands, who often accompanied him in his early years, also probably added to his public relations problems. The Vikings were not popular in Wales.

94 Maund, K. L., *Ireland*, pp.146–7. The biography of Gruffudd ap Cynan states that Caradog brought Norman archers with him in

his attack on Rhys ap Tewdwr in 1081. Evans, *A Mediaeval Prince*, pp.35, 66.

95 On this element in the Chronicles, see Maund, K. L., 'Owain ap Cadwgan: a Rebel Revisited', *Haskins Society Journal* 13 (1999), pp.65–74, pp.72–4.

96 The pro-Powys *Brutiau* claim that the entire warband of Rhys ab Owain fell in the battle with Trahaearn, but this is very likely an exaggeration. *ByT* (Pen. 20) [1076–1078]; *ByT* (RB) [–1078]; *BS* [1076–1078]

97 It is, of course, impossible to know how old either Cadell or Tewdwr were when they had their children – men in medieval Wales could and did father children from their teens until late in life. However, the early eleventh century was a turbulent period in Deheubarth, and, as members of the royal line, Cadell and Tewdwr will have been expected to put their lives at risk in battle in their youth. We cannot be sure either of them lived to any great age.

98 There were settlements of Scandinavians in several places in Ireland, notably Dublin, Wexford, Waterford, Limerick and Cork. They had also settled on the Isle of Man and in the Western Isles, and the kings of Norway took an interest in these territories. As with all topics relating to Vikings, the literature is extensive, but a good starting place for their history in the Irish Sea province is Smyth, A. P., *Scandinavian York and Dublin: the History and Archaeology of two related Viking Kingdoms* 2 vols (Dublin, 1975–9).

99 Trahaearn had sons of his own, but they were probably still young children at this time. Their main period of activity lies in the first quarter of the twelfth century. Bleddyn ap Cynfyn had had a number of sons, and these may have been close to adulthood by 1081 – three of them became active from 1088. Meilyr's father had died in 1069 and it is likely he was the eldest of the pool of heirs and kinsmen available to Trahaearn.

100 This is not the place to rehearse the issues surrounding Trahaearn. The traditional view of him may be found in Lloyd, *A History*, II, pp.378–85; a more modern assessment is given in

Maund, K. L., 'Trahaearn ap Caradog: Legitimate Usurper?', *Welsh History Review* 13 (1986–7), pp.468–76.

101 On Gruffudd ap Cynan, see Lloyd, *A History*, II pp.379–92, pp.404–5, 408–411; R. R. Davies, *Conquest, Coexistence and Change: Wales 1063–1415* (Oxford, 1987), pp.43–5; Maund, K. L., ed., *Gruffudd ap Cynan: A Collaborative Biography* (Woodbridge, 1996); Maund, K. L., *Ireland*, pp.82–90, pp.149–51, pp.153–5, pp.171–82; Maund, K. L., *Welsh Kings*, pp.78–80, pp.83–5, pp.93–8.

102 'brenhin brenhined Kemry' Evans, *A Mediaeval Prince*, pp.35, p.66.

103 I have discussed this battle at length elsewhere: Maund, K. L., 'Trahaearn'; Maund, K.L., *Ireland*, pp.34–6; Maund, K.L., *Welsh Kings*, pp.78–80. See also the illuminating discussion of Babcock, 'Rhys', pp.24–6.

104 Jones, ed. and trans., *Brut y Tywysogyon Red Book of Hergest version*, pp.30–31, [–1081]. Menevia, or *Mynyw*, is the Welsh word for St Davids. William the Conqueror was an illegitimate child: the use of 'bastard' here is thus accurate. By referring to this, however, the writer of this entry almost certainly meant to be critical or insulting.

105 For instance, Gruffudd ap Llywelyn came to meet representatives of Edward the Confessor at Hereford to make peace in 1055.

106 An excellent discussion of William's journey to Wales is found in Babcock, 'Rhys', pp.26–7.

107 Maund, K. L., *Ireland*, pp.139–40.

108 *Domesday Book* gen. ed. Morris, 179b.

109 It was not at all unusual for Welsh kings to have several wives, and not necessarily serially.

110 *ByT* (Pen. 20) [1113–1115]; *ByT* (RB) [1113–1116]; *BS* [1113–1116].

111 Of her sons both Maurice and David died in 1176, when they were old men. Robert, probably her youngest son, died in around 1182. Henry, who, as will be argued later in this book, was probably her first child, was killed in 1157.

112 The date of her marriage and her age at the time will be discussed further in chapter 3.

113 It was, however considered inappropriate for her to bear a child before the age of fourteen. Jenkins, *Law*, p.132.

114 McAll, C., 'The Normal Paradigms of a Woman's Life in the Irish and Welsh Texts', in Jenkins, D. and Owen, M. E., eds, *The Welsh Law of Women* (Cardiff, 1980), pp.7–22, p.8.

115 The wife in question was Joanna, married to Llywelyn the Great, who may have been something of a special case. She was the illegitimate – but favoured – daughter of King John. An earlier prince in Gwynedd, Llywelyn's uncle Dafydd ab Owain, had married another illegitimate royal child, Emma of Anjou, daughter of Henry II, but she is a much more shadowy figure who seems not to have exercised much influence over her father or husband. In the three known surviving charters granted by Emma, she is referred to as 'wife of Dafydd ab Owain'. Joanna in her extant letters uses the title 'Lady of Wales'. Maund, K. L., *Handlist of the Acts of Native Welsh Rulers 1132–1283* (Cardiff, 1996) nos 117, 119, 121, 340, 468.

116 On the household of the king's wife, see Robin Chapman Stacey, 'King, Queen and *Edling* in the Laws of Court', in Charles-Edwards et al., eds *The Welsh Kings* 29–62, pp.53–62.

117 The *Life of Samson* is the earliest of the extant Saints' Lives with a Welsh context, having been composed probably by the mid-ninth century at the latest, and perhaps as early as the seventh century.

118 Lloyd-Morgan, C., 'More written about than writing? Welsh women and the written word', in Pryce, H., ed., *Literacy in Medieval Celtic Societies* (Cambridge, 1998), 149–65, p.151.

119 Evans, *A Medieval Prince*, pp.28, 58.

120 Gantz, *Mabinogion*, p.65.

121 Gantz, *Mabinogion*, p.109.

122 The legal standing and values of women will be considered in more detail in chapter 2.

123 For a discussion of these, see Jenkins, D., 'Property Interests in the Classical Welsh Law of Women' in Jenkins and Owen, eds, *Women*, pp.69–92.

124 Jenkins, *Law*, p.54,

125 The question of monastic literacy is more complex. The traditional Welsh monastic churches, known as *clas* churches, were essentially

hereditary property with a population of people who in many ways conducted their lives like any peasant farmer. Some of the men in such communities were probably literate, but it would be a mistake to assume that they all were.

126 This is another difference between cultural practice in Wales and Ireland.

127 See the discussion by Lloyd-Morgan, 'More written about,' cited in note 118 above.

128 Babcock, 'Rhys', pp.28–9, p.31.

129 Robert Curthose inherited the duchy of Normandy: this was the senior holding from the point of view of the Conqueror, as it was the one he had held first. It was thus the right of the eldest son. England, as a conquered territory, was not part of the patrimonial inheritance, and thus could be left to the second son. William's third son, Henry – the future Henry I – inherited a considerable sum of money, but no land.

130 On this rebellion see Frank Barlow, *William Rufus* (London, 1983), pp.53–98.

131 The most accessible ones would have been Waterford and Wexford.

132 Williams, J., ed., *Annales Cambriae* (London 1860) (C-text) s. a. 1087; *ByT* (Pen. 20) [1086–1088].

133 *AC* (B) s. a. 1087; *AC* (C) s. a. 1087; *ByT* (Pen. 20) [1086–1088]; *ByT* (RB) [–1088]; *BS* [–1088].

134 *AC* (B) s. a. 1087; *AC* (C) s. a. 1087.

135 *ByT* (Pen. 20) [1113–1116]; *ByT* (RB) [1112–1116]; *BS* [1113–1116]

136 On this, see Maund, K. L., 'Owain', pp. 72–4.

137 *ByT* (Pen. 20), [1113–1116]; *ByT* (RB) [1113–1116] and *BS* [1113–1116].

138 *AC* (B) s. a. 1089; *AC* (C) s. a. 1089; *ByT* (Pen. 20) [1089–1091]; *ByT* (RB) [–1091]; *BS* [1089–1091].

139 Babcock, 'Rhys', pp.31–5.

140 Lynn H. Nelson, *The Normans in South Wales 1070 – 1171* (Austin, Texas 1966), p.82, p.87; Lloyd, *A History*, II, pp.397 & n. 135; David

Walker, *The Normans in South Wales* (Swansea 1977), p.34.

141 Nelson, *Normans*, pp.84–5; Walker, *Normans*, p.34.

142 Nelson, *Normans*, pp.86–7.

143 Bernard seems to have joined the rebellion because of his father-in-law; Nelson, *Normans*, p.88.

144 *JW* s. a. 1093.

145 *ByT* (Pen. 20) [1091–1093].

CHAPTER 2

1 Jenkins, *Law*, p.131.

2 We do not possess a direct statement of Nest's views on this, but her grandson Gerald of Wales demonstrates notable affection for the Welsh and pride in his Welsh ancestry, which he must surely have learnt from his mother, Angharad, and she from her mother, Nest.

3 *ByT* (Pen. 20) [1112–1115]; *ByT* (RB) [1112–1116]; *BS* [1112–1115].

4 Two of Cadwgan's brothers, Madog and Rhirid had died in battle in 1088, but he had three others that we know of (Iorwerth, Maredudd and the shadowy Llywarch), all of whom must have been younger than him. He was eventually to have seven known sons by five different women, some of whom were probably born before 1093. His brother Rhirid, (d.1088) had left two sons, also. The Line of Bleddyn was notably prolific in its early generations.

5 Gerald, *Journey*, book 1, chap.12, trans. Thorpe, p.148; *Opera*, vol.6, p.89.

6 Gerald, *Journey*, trans. Thorpe, pp.148–9.

7 Ifor Rowlands, 'The Making of the March: Aspects of the Norman Settlement in Dyfed', *Proceedings of the Battle Conference on Anglo-Norman Studies* 3 (1980), 142–157, pp.142–3.

8 *ByT* (RB) [1112–1115]; *BS* [1112–1116].

9 This idea can be found elaborated in Markale, J., *La Femme Celte* (1972), translated by Mygind, A., as *Women of the Celts* (1975); Peter Beresford Ellis, *Celtic Women* (London, 1995). It also appears in innumerable works of fiction.

10 Simon James, *The Atlantic Celts: Ancient People or Modern Invention?* (London, 1999).

11 A selection of late antique authors' accounts of women belonging to groups sometimes considered as Celtic can be found in translation in Philip Freeman, *War, Women and Druids: Eyewitness reports and early accounts of the Ancient Celts* (Austin, Texas 2002), pp. 53–9.

12 I owe this observation to the Scottish writer, Jane Carnall.

13 The argument that the bulk of the male population assisted the incoming priests out of jealousy or a self-interested desire for dominance strikes me as cynical to an unkind degree.

14 In their extant form the earliest of the law codes date probably from the later twelfth century. This is a little after Nest's time, but the material does not show a high degree of influence from Norman or Angevin practice, and, indeed, is generally conservative in nature. It may thus throw some light on the way native law viewed women in Wales in Nest's lifetime.

15 The variant versions of these have been published in Jenkins and Owen, *Women*, pp. 132–79.

16 Foetuses were treated as being of equal value, as nothing was known of their sex prior to birth. McAll, 'Normal Paradigms', in Jenkins and Owen, *Women*, pp. 7–22.

17 Jenkins, *Law*, p. 47. This does not mean that she had to possess a brother: the law here is predicated on what the brother's value would be, regardless of his actual existence.

18 Jenkins, *Law*, pp. 131–2. The law codes observe that while a girl should remain at her father's platter until she is 12 to 14 years old, at which point 'even if she does not take a husband she is entitled to control what is hers'. (p. 132). This implies at least that not all girls were married off at 14.

19 Jenkins, *Law*, p. 30 (queen's handmaid); p. 37 (bakeress); p. 39 (laundress).

20 Jenkins, *Law*, p. 37.

21 On these, and other marriage alliances, see Roderick, A. J., 'Marriage and Politics in Wales 1066–1282', *Welsh History Review* 4 (1968), pp. 3–20.

22 Jenkins, *Law*, p.49.

23 The laws contain provision for rape, but what became of an unmarried girl who lost her virginity to such an attack is not dealt with.

24 The name translates literally as 'Island of the Mighty'.

25 Gantz, *Mabinogion*, p.68.

26 *ByT* (Pen. 20) [1113–1116]; *ByT* (RB) [1113–1117]; *BS* [1113–1116].

27 *ByT* (Pen. 20) [1122–1125]; *ByT* (RB) [1122–1125]; *BS* [1122–1125].

28 The form of adulthood available to women was, however, limited.

29 Jenkins, *Law*, p.46.

30 Jenkins, *Law*, p.53.

31 Jenkins, *Law*, p.45.

32 See also Davies, R. R., 'The Status of Women and the Practice of Marriage in late-medieval Wales', in Jenkinsand Owen, *Women*, 93–114.

33 Jenkins, *Law*, pp.107–10

34 Jenkins, *Law*, pp.98–100.

35 Jenkins, *Law*, p.54.

36 Gantz, *Mabinogion*, p.73.

37 Gantz, *Mabinogion*, p.77.

38 Gantz, *Mabinogion*, p.85.

39 Gantz, *Mabinogion*, pp.90–3.

40 Gantz, *Mabinogion*, pp.106–11.

CHAPTER 3

1 The standard work on William remains Douglas, D. C., *William the Conqueror* (London, 1963).

2 On this, see Nelson, *Normans*, pp.66–9.

3 He also had one son, Everard, from his second marriage, who was younger than the others. He would become a royal chaplain to William Rufus and Henry I.

4 It is unlikely he felt any strong attachment to the idea of male primogeniture (inheritance of the entire patrimony by the eldest son) given the disposition he made of his own lands.

5 For these territories, see Nelson, *Normans*, pp.67–9.

6 Davies, *Conquest*, p.30.

7 There were Welshmen involved in the resistance to William Rufus in 1088: it is not impossible that these included Cadwgan ab Bleddyn, who stood to gain from prolongation of conflict within England.

8 I have argued elsewhere that Cadwgan's main interest may have been in the domination of Ceredigion. See Maund, K. L., 'Owain', p.17.

9 Orderic Vitalis, *The Ecclesiastical History of Orderic Vitalis*, ed. and trans. Chibnall, M., 6 vols (Oxford, 1968–80), vol.II, book IV, p.261.

10 *OV*, book 4, ed. and trans Chibnall, II, pp.135–7.

11 *OV*, book 8, ed and trans Chibnall, IV, pp.302–3.

12 Rowlands, 'Dyfed', p.145.

13 A useful summary as far as Anglo-Saxon women are concerned is given by Pauline Stafford, 'Women and the Norman Conquest', *Transactions of the Royal Historical Society* ser. 6, vol.4 (1994), 221–49. As far as women in the Celtic speaking countries are concerned, the charge is more indirect: in popular works on such women, it is implied that through a combination of Christianisation and colonisation, female rights were eroded.

14 Stafford, 'Women', pp.221–9.

15 Davies, W., 'Celtic Women in the Early Middle Ages', in Averil Cameron and Amélie Kuhrt, eds, *Images of Women in Antiquity* (London, 1993), pp.145–66.

16 *English Historical Documents vol.II: 1042–1189* eds, Douglas, D. C. and Greenaway, G.W., 2nd ed. (London 1981), p.433.

17 The importance of these issues in relation to women is discussed in Searle, E., 'Women and the legitimisation of succession of succession at the Norman Conquest', *Proceedings of the Battle Conference on Anglo-Norman Studies* 3 (1980), pp.159–70 and pp.226–9.

18 See previous note.

19 Hollister, C.W., *Henry I* (New Haven, 2001), pp.126–8.

20 Coss, P., *The Lady in Medieval England 1000–1500* (Stroud, 1998), p.18; Searle, 'Women', p.160.

21 As was argued in chapter 2, it is inappropriate and misleading to introduce figures from early Irish legend to a discussion of the political role of women in Wales.

22 There is not space in this book for a detailed account of Anglo-Norman women. Excellent discussions may be found in Coss, *Lady* and in Henrietta Leyser, *Medieval Women* (London, 1995).

23 Coss, *Lady*, p.29.

24 Bosanquet, G., trans., *Eadmer's History of Recent Events in England* (London, 1964), p.196.

25 It never fell to attackers during its functional life.

26 For a detailed account, see Maund, K. L., *Ireland*, pp.148–53.

27 Searle, 'Women', pp.165–6.

28 Searle, 'Women', pp.166–7; Lois L. Huneycutt, *Matilda of Scotland: a study in Medieval Queenship* (Woodbridge, 2003), pp.17–25.

29 Searle, 'Women', pp.167–9; Leyser, *Medieval Women*, pp.81–2.

30 Coss, *Lady*, pp.23–3; Searle, 'Women', pp.159–62; Leyser, *Medieval Women*, pp.87–8.

31 The classic study is that of Davies, R. R., *Lordship and Society in the March of Wales 1282–1400* (Oxford, 1978).

32 The literature on the Normans in Ireland is immense. A good starting place is Flanagan, M. T., *Irish Society, Anglo-Norman Settlement Angevin Kingship* (Oxford, 1989).

33 Maund, K. L., *Welsh Kings*, p.147.

34 On the Corbet family, see Meisel, J., *Barons of the Welsh Frontier: the Corbet, Pantulf and Fitz Warin Families 1066–1272* (Lincoln, Nebraska, 1980).

35 'Henry I's Illegitimate Children', in *The Complete Peerage* ed. G. E. C. vol.XI, appendix D, 105–121, pp.107–8.

36 Meisel, *Barons*, pp.3–6.

37 Mason, J. F.A., 'Roger of Montgomery and his Sons', *Transactions of the Royal Historical Society* 5th ser., Vol.13 (1963), 1–28, pp.17–18.

38 This conspiracy centred on the actions of Robert Mowbray, earl of Northumberland, and may have been aimed at deposing Rufus in favour of his cousin Stephen of Aumale, son of Rufus' sister Adelaide. Frank Barlow, *William Rufus* (London, 1983), pp.346–354.

39 *ASC* [E] s. a. 1095.

40 *ASC* [E] s. a. 1095.

41 This is also the conclusion of Professor Barlow, *William Rufus*, p.354.

42 This is the Nest who was the grand-daughter of the great Gruffudd ap Llywelyn. Gruffudd's mother was Angharad ap Maredudd, of the royal house of Deheubarth. Angharad had been the daughter of Nest's great-great-grand-uncle, Maredudd ab Owain (d.999). This was remote by any standards.

43 *OV*, ed. and trans., Chibnall, book 8, p.189.

44 See the discussion by Barlow, *William Rufus*, pp.103–15.

45 For a detailed discussion of the date and place of his birth, see Hollister, *Henry*, p.31.

46 The birth order was Robert (Curthose), Richard, William (Rufus), Henry. Richard was killed in an accident in the New Forest in 1075, thus predeceasing his father.

47 See Hollister, *Henry*, pp.39–40.

48 This is discussed in detail by Hollister, *Henry*, pp.57–65.

49 Hollister, *Henry*, pp.69–76.

50 Hollister, *Henry*, pp.76–83.

51 Hollister, *Henry*, pp.85–7.

52 Hollister, *Henry*, pp.93–7.

53 Hollister, *Henry*, p.98.

54 Van Houts, E. M. C., ed. and trans., *Gesta Normannorum Ducum of William of Jumièges, Orderic Vitalis and Robert of Torigni*, 2 vols (Oxford, 1992–95), vol.2, pp.210–13.

55 William Rufus was killed in a hunting accident on 2 August 1100, and Henry crowned three days later, on 5 August. He married the following November, and remained in England until 1104.

56 William of Malmesbury, *Gesta Regum Anglorum The History of the English Kings* ed. and trans. R. A. B. Mynors, R. M. Thompson and M. Winterbottom, 2 vols (Oxford, 1998–9), I, pp.744–5.

57 Gerald, *Autobiography*, book I, ch.1; *Journey.*, book II, ch.7. *The Autobiography of Gerald of* Wales, ed. and trans. H. E. Butler (new ed. Woodbridge, 2005), p.35; *Journey* trans. Thorpe, p.189; *Opera*, vol.1, p.21; vol.6, p.130.

58 Gantz, *Mabinogion*, p.48.

59 Gantz, *Mabinogion*, p.49.

60 Gantz, *Mabinogion*, p.54.

61 Gantz, *Mabinogion*, p.68.

62 Gantz, *Mabinogion*, pp.151–2.

63 Burgess, G. S. and Busby, K., trans., *The Lais of Marie de France*, (Harmondsworth, 1986) 'Lanval', p. 80.

64 Chrétien de Troyes, *Arthurian Romances* trans. Owen, D. D. R. (London, 1987). In *Cligés,* Soredamors, the mother of the hero, is blonde (p.106), for instance.

65 Giraldus Cambrensis [Gerald of Wales], *Expugnatio Hibernica The Conquest of Ireland*, ed. and trans. Scott, A. B. and Martin, F. X. (Dublin, 1978), pp.118–21.

66 Gerald, *Conquest*, ed. and trans. Scott and Martin, pp.152–3.

67 David Crouch, 'Robert of Gloucester's mother and sexual politics in Norman Oxfordshire', *Historical Research* vol.72 no. 179 (October 1999), pp.323–33.

68 Crouch, 'Robert', p.331.

69 Crouch, 'Robert', pp.323, 329.

70 Crouch, 'Robert', pp.329, 331.

71 Crouch, 'Robert', p.330.

72 'Henry I's Illegitimate Children', pp.107–8.

73 Meisel, *Barons*, p.4.

74 'Henry I's Illegitimate Children', pp.110–11.

75 William of Malmesbury, *Gesta*, ed. and trans. Mynors et al., I, pp.744–5.

76 Searle, 'Women', p.169. There is further useful discussion of this matter in Charlotte Newman, *The Anglo-Norman Nobility in the*

Reign of Henry I (Philadephia, 1988), pp.55–9; Hollister, *Henry* pp.41–5.

77 See previous note.

78 'Henry I's Illegitimate Children', p.118.

79 'Henry I's Illegitimate Children', pp.112–3.

80 'Henry I's Illegitimate Children', p.114.

81 Lloyd, *A History*, II, pp.686–7; p.696–701; Davies, *Conquest*, pp.249–50; pp.300–1.

82 Douglas, *William the Conqueror*, pp.37–44; pp.47–80.

83 Hollister, *Henry*, p.42 and n.73.

84 Hollister, *Henry*, p.44.

85 Newman, *Nobility*, p.58.

CHAPTER 4

1 Hollister, *Henry*, p.85, pp.102–9.

2 Hollister, *Henry*, pp.126–8. On Edith-Matilda, see Huneycutt, *Matilda*.

3 Mason, 'Roger', p.19.

4 Mason, 'Roger', p.19.

5 *OV*, book VIII ed. and trans. Chibnall, IV, pp.158–61.

6 Hollister, *Henry*, p.132.

7 Hollister, *Henry*, pp.139–45.

8 Hollister, *Henry*, p.156.

9 *ByT* (Pen. 20) [1100–1102]; *ByT* (RB) [1100–1102]; *BS* [1100–1102].

10 *ByT* (Pen 20) [1100–1102] trans. Jones, p.23.

11 In 1088 and 1093.

12 Nelson, *Normans*, p.119. Nelson rather overestimates the power of Cadwgan's former associate Gruffudd ap Cynan here, suggesting that the latter was 'allowed' Gwynedd apparently without conditions. Cadwgan was in fact by the far the more powerful of the two Welsh leaders and Robert will have been aware that in order to avoid further military activities on his borders, he needed peace with Cadwgan.

13 *ByT* (Pen. 20) [1100–1102]; *ByT* (RB) [1100–1102]; *BS* [1100–1102].

14 This rebellion is noted in most of the extant sources: in addition to the Welsh chronicles listed in the previous note, see *OV*, Book XI, ed. and trans. Chibnall, VI, p.32; *JW* [1102]; *ASC* (E) [1101=1102]

15 Maredudd is found supporting Cadwgan on through the first decades of the twelfth century.

16 The wording of the *Brutiau* might support this interpretation, as it describes Iorwerth's actions as avenging wrongs done to the Welsh of Powys by Robert and his family. It should, however, be born in mind that this section of the *Brutiau* was probably subjected to some degree of re-writing after these events and that the account is coloured by the attitude of the compiler or composer of this section, who seems to have been staunchly anti-Norman. *ByT* (Pen. 20) [1100–1102]; *ByT* (RB) [1100–1102]; *BS* [1100–1102].

17 *OV*, book XI, ed. and trans. Chibnall, VI, pp.30–1. The rebellion is noted by *ASC* (E) 1101=1102, *JW* 1102 and the Welsh chronicles cited above and there are minor variations in the details of its progress and Henry's response. See also Hollister, *Henry*, pp.154–63.

18 The main discussion of Arnulf's future career remains E. Curtis, 'Muirchertach O'Brien, High King of Ireland, and his Norman Son-in-Law, Arnulf de Montgomery *c.*1100', *Journal of the Royal Society of the Antiquaries of Ireland,* series 6, no. 11–12 (1921–22), 116–24.

19 *OV*, book XI, ed. and trans. Chibnall, VI, 50–1.

20 *ByT* (Pen. 20) [1095 – 1097]; *ByT* (RB) [1093 – 1097]; *BS* [1095 – 1097]. For the enmity of the bishop, see Gerald, *Journey*, book I, ch.12, trans. Thorpe, p.148; *Opera*, vol.6, p.90.

21 Gerald, *Journey*, book I, ch.12, trans. Thorpe, pp.148–9; *Opera*, vol.6, p.89.

22 Newman, *Anglo-Norman Nobility*, p.4.

23 Green, J.A., *The Government of England under Henry I* (Cambridge 1986), p.254.

24 Green, *Government*, p.254.

25 It is more likely that Nest married Gerald at Henry's behest in or after 1102 than that she did so at an earlier date under Arnulf's influence. It is hard to see why Arnulf would allow a young woman with her family links to marry his constable.

26 Pettifer, A., *Welsh Castles* (Woodbridge, 2000), p.155.

27 Davies, R. R., 'Henry I and Wales', in Henry Mayr-Harting and R. I.. Moore, eds, *Studies in Medieval History Presented to R. H. C. Davis* (London, 1985), 133–47, p.136.

28 The date of the beginning of this colony is uncertain. John of Worcester places it in 1111 (*JW* s.a. 1111); the *Brutiau* in 1108: *ByT* (Pen. 20) [1105–1108], *ByT* (RB) [1104–1108], *BS* [1105–1108]. On this settlement, see Davies, *Conquest*, pp.98–9, pp.159–60.

29 *ByT* (Pen. 20), [1105–1108], trans. Jones.

30 *ByT* (Pen. 20), [1129–1132], trans. Jones.

31 Maund, K. L., 'Owain', pp.72–3.

32 I have suggested that the prose tale elements may have taken their current form at some point in the reign of and under the influence, if not the direction of Owain Cyfeiliog, grandson of Maredudd ab Bleddyn and ruler of southern Powys 1160–1197; Maund, K. L., 'Owain', p.79.

33 Notably in Lloyd, *A History*, II, p.417, pp.419–20.

34 His wives or concubines included the daughter of Picot de Sai, a vassal of the earls of Shrewsbury.

35 On Cadwgan and Ceredigion, see Maund, K. L., 'Owain', p.71.

36 *ByT* (Pen. 20) [1106–1109].

37 *ByT* (Pen. 20) [1106–1109].

38 Gerald, *Autobiography*, book I, ch.9; trans. Butler, p.83; *Opera*, vol.1, pp.58–9.

39 David Crouch, 'Nest', *Oxford Dictionary of National Biography* vol.40, eds Matthew, H. G. C. and Harrison, B. (Oxford, 2004), pp. 441–2.

40 Crouch, 'Nest', p.441.

41 For more detailed discussion of the rebellion, see Davies, 'Henry I and Wales'; Maund, K. L., 'Owain'.

42 *ByT* (Pen. 20) [1112–1115], trans. Jones, p.39.

43 See the valuable discussion in Babcock, R. S., 'Imbeciles and Normans: The *Ynfydion* of Gruffudd ap Rhys Reconsidered', *The Haskins Society Journal* 4 (1992), pp.1–9.

44 Babcock, 'Imbeciles', pp.1–2.

45 *ByT* (Pen. 20) [1112–1115]; *ByT* (RB) [1112–1115]; *BS* [1112–1115].

46 Babcock, 'Imbeciles', p.4.

47 The assault on Aberystwyth was to prove his undoing.

48 The nature of his support is discussed by Babcock, 'Imbeciles', pp.5–9. Rhydderch joined his nephew part way through 1116: *ByT* (Pen. 20) [111 1–1116]; *ByT* (RB) [1113–1116]; *BS* [1113–1116].

49 The description in the Chronicles does not make it clear whom Owain had been fighting, but the implication seems to be that he had concluded that the local population were sheltering or aiding Gruffudd ap Rhys.

50 *ByT* (Pen. 20) [1113–1116], trans. Jones, p.45.

51 These would cause Henry I to make a second expedition against Wales in 1121.

52 On Rhys, see Roger Turvey, *The Lord Rhys* (Llandysul 1997); Lloyd, *A History*, II, pp.536–72; Davies, *Conquest*, pp.218–24; Maund, K. L., *Welsh Kings*, pp.102–12.

53 *ByT* (Pen. 20) [1124–1127]; *ByT* (RB) [1124–1127]; *BS* [1124–1127].

54 Crouch, 'Nest', p.442.

55 Crouch, 'Nest', p.442; Roderick, 'Marriage', p.6 and n. 3..

56 On the problems faced by widows in Anglo-Norman England, see Newman, *Nobility*, pp.44–5; Coss, *Lady*, pp.26–30.

57 Gerald, *Conquest*, book I c. 26; trans. Scott et al., pp.86–7; *Opera*, vol.5, pp.271–2.

58 Gerald, *Journey*., book I ch.9; trans. Thorpe, p.137; *Opera*, vol.6, p.79.

59 His father was William fitz Gerald.

SELECT BIBLIOGRAPHY

Barlow, F., *William Rufus* (London, 1983).

Cameron, A. and Kuhrt, A., eds, *Images of Women in Antiquity* (London, 1993).

Charles-Edwards, T. M., Owen, M. E. and Russell, P., edd., *The Welsh King and His Court* (Cardiff, 2000).

Coss, P., *The Lady in Medieval England 1000–1500* (Stroud, 1998).

Davies, R. R., *Conquest, Coexistence and Change: Wales 1066–1415* (Oxford, 1987) [paperback edition retitled *Age of Conquest: Wales 1066–1415* (Oxford, 1990)].

Davies, W., *Wales in the Early Middle Ages* (Leicester, 1982).

Douglas, D. C., *William the Conqueror* (London, 1963).

Gantz, J., trans., *The Mabinogion* (Harmondsworth, 1976).

Gerald of Wales, trans. Thorpe, L., *The Journey through Wales and the Description of Wales*, (Harmondsworth, 1978).

Gerald of Wales, ed. and trans. Butler, H. E. *Autobiography* (new revised edition Woodbridge, 2005).

Gerald of Wales, eds and trans. Scott, A. B. and Martin, F. X., *Expugnatio Hibernica: the Conquest of Ireland* (Dublin, 1978).

Green, J. A., *The Government of England under Henry I* (Cambridge, 1986).

Hollister, C. W., *Henry I* (New Haven, 2001).

Huneycutt, L. L., *Matilda of Scotland: a study in Medieval Queenship*

(Woodbridge, 2003).

Jenkins, D., trans., *The Law of Hywel Dda: Law Texts from Medieval Wales* (Llandysul, 1986).

Jenkins, D., *The Law of Hywel Dda* (Llandysul, 1990).

Jenkins, D. and Owen, M. E., eds, *The Welsh Law of Women* (Cardiff, 1980).

Leyser, H., *Medieval Women* (London, 1995).

Lloyd, J. E., *A History of Wales from the earliest times to the Edwardian conquest*, 2 vols. (3rd edition, London, 1939).

Maund, K. L., *The Welsh Kings: the medieval rulers of Wales* (Stroud, 2000).

Maund, K. L., *Ireland, Wales and England in the Eleventh Century* (Woodbridge, 1991).

Meisel, J., *Barons of the Welsh Frontier: the Corbet, Pantulf and Fitz Warin Families 1066–1272* (Lincoln, Nebraska, 1980).

Nelson, L. H., *The Normans in South Wales 1070–1171* (Austin, Texas, 1966).

Newman, C., *The Anglo-Norman Nobility in the Reign of Henry I* (Philadephia, 1988).

Further reading can be found in the notes.

LIST OF ILLUSTRATIONS

LIST OF FIGURES

GENEALOGICAL TABLES
AND MAPS

Fig.1 Nest's Wales

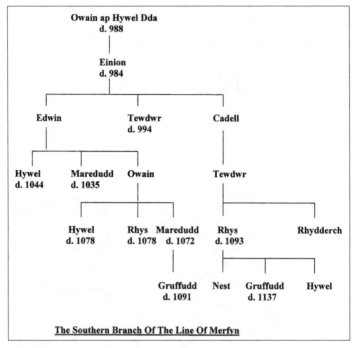

Fig.2 The southern branch of the line of Merfyn

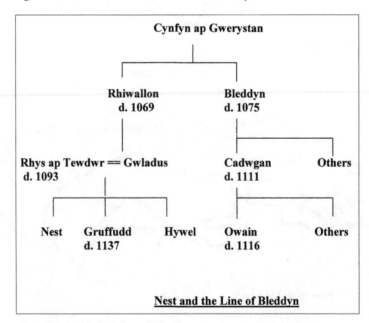

Fig.3 Nest and the Line of Bleddyn

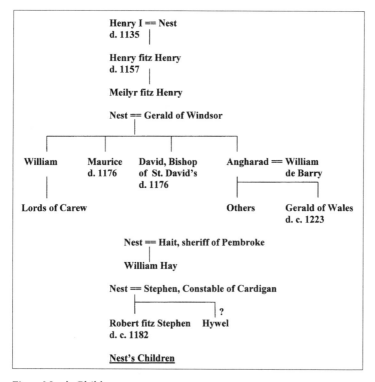

Fig.4 Nest's Children

INDEX

TEMPUS – REVEALING HISTORY

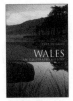   

Wales: An Illustrated History
PRYS MORGAN (ED.)

'Masterly... this well-illustrated narrative of Wales from prehistory to the present day can be strongly recommended'
BBC History Magazine

£17.99
0 7524 2970 1

Welsh Kings: Warriors, Warlords and Princes
KARI MAUND

'A must for all lovers of Welsh history'
South Wales Argus

£10.99
0 7524 2973 6

Merthyr Tydfil:
Iron Metropolis – Life in a Welsh Industrial Town
KEITH STRANGE

£17.99
0 7524 3451 9

The Welsh Wars of Independence
DAVID MOORE

'Beautifully written, subtle and remarkably perceptive... a major re-examination of a thousand years of Welsh history'
John Davies

£12.99
978 07524 4128 3

FORTHCOMING WELSH HISTORY FROM TEMPUS

Tudor Wales
From Owain Glyn Dwr to the Spanish Armada
MATTHEW GRIFFITHS

Welsh Witches and Wizards
A History of Magic and Witchcraft in Wales
RICHARD SUGGETT

The Renaissance in Wales
NIA POWELL

The Welsh Bible
ERYN WHITE

Wales at War
The Experience of the Second World War in Wales
STUART BROOMFIELD

Music in Wales: A History
LYNN DAVIES

If you are interested in purchasing other books published by Tempus, or in case you have difficulty finding any Tempus books in your local bookshop, you can also place orders directly through our website
www.tempus-publishing.com